# AND SHE AROSE AS A MOTHER

## Amma

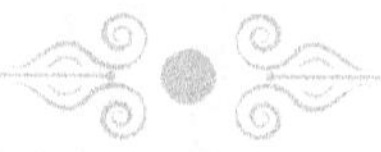

# AND SHE AROSE AS A MOTHER



*Contact Author on:*
ammagrace98@gmail.com

*Book Layout by*
INDES PROCOM LIMITED
Email: info@indesprocom.com
Website: www.indesprocom.com

*Cover Credit:*
Richard Opoku Agyeman
Co-Founder/Creative Director
ACUTE FORMULA LLC
info@acuteformula.net

# Contents:

# Dedication

THIS BOOK IS HUMBLY DEDICATED TO DR. MRS. ABIGAIL KYEI AND  MRS. HANNAH ACQUAH-SAMPSON. THEIR MOTHERLY LEADERSHIP HAS BEEN A GUIDING LIGHT DURING MY FORMATIVE YEARS, INSTILLING HOPE AND PROVIDING DIRECTION. I HONOR THEM, AND ALL WOMEN WHO, WITH UNWAVERING COMMITMENT AND COMPASSION, SERVE HUMANITY. THEIR LEGACY OF KINDNESS CONTINUES TO MAKE A SIGNIFICANT IMPACT IN THE WORLD.

ALSO, THIS DEDICATION EXTENDS TO ALL WOMEN WHO, FOR REASONS KNOWN ONLY TO THEM AND GOD, DO NOT HAVE THEIR OWN CHILDREN BUT HARBOR A DEEP-SEATED DESIRE FOR MOTHERHOOD. YOU ARE SEEN, YOU ARE HEARD, AND YOU ARE LOVED.

MAY THIS BOOK SERVE AS A BEACON OF HOPE, A TESTAMENT TO THE STRENGTH OF WOMANHOOD, AND A TRIBUTE TO THE UNYIELDING SPIRIT OF MOTHERHOOD THAT RESIDES IN EACH ONE OF YOU. IT IS A CELEBRATION OF YOUR RESILIENCE, YOUR COURAGE, AND YOUR UNDYING LOVE. MAY IT INSPIRE AND UPLIFT YOU, ACKNOWLEDGING YOUR INVALUABLE CONTRIBUTIONS TO THE WORLD. AS YOU, DELICATELY TURN THE PAGES OF THIS BOOK, MAY IT SERVE AS A DIVINE AFFIRMATION, EMPOWERING YOU WHO HARBOR THE DESIRE TO EMBRACE MOTHERHOOD, TO ACTUALIZE YOUR DREAMS.

# Foreword

In the pages of Amma's book, "And She Arose as a Mother," we, as women, are invited to explore a profound concept: the expansion of motherhood beyond the confines of family, reaching out to encompass all those we encounter in our journey through life. This is not merely a book but a call to action, a plea for us to recognize and embrace our inherent capacity to nurture, guide, and positively impact the lives of those around us.

Our world is teeming with individuals yearning for direction, for purpose, for a beacon to illuminate the opportunities that lie before them. This book serves as a testament to the power of guidance, the transformative potential of providing focus, and fostering fruitfulness in the lives of others. It is a reminder that we, as women, are all capable of lighting the path for those who may be struggling to find their way.

This is not just a privilege but a God-given responsibility, a gift that must be nurtured and cherished. We are all mothers in our own right, regardless of gender or age. We mother our peers, our elders, and sometimes even those younger than us. In this context, motherhood transcends traditional definitions to embody the act of mentoring, of nurturing the inherent goodness within individuals until they reach full maturity and realize their true potential.

This book is a celebration of that process, a tribute to the rewarding journey of guiding others toward their own self-discovery. It is a testament to the power of 'mothering' in its broadest sense and a guide to how we, as women, can play our part in bettering the world, one person at a time.

Amma's book is a clarion call for us all to mature into mentors, take the concept of motherhood to a higher level, and recognize the profound

impact we can have on the lives of those we come into contact with. It is, indeed, a rewarding journey, and this book is a valuable companion for all who embark upon it.

"And She Arose as a Mother" is a tribute to the power of womanhood, as embodied by all women. It is not a political commentary or an endorsement of any specific political ideology. Instead, it explores womanhood's universally admired and respected qualities - love, sacrifice, resilience, and loyalty.

The narrative draws inspiration from the public life and career of women who have made significant contributions to society, including Kamala Harris, whose maternal leadership has been a beacon of hope and inspiration. However, it is not a biography. It does not delve into personal lives or pass judgment on private decisions. Instead, it focuses on their public persona and their role as female figures in various fields.

The book also acknowledges the diversity of womanhood. It recognizes that mothers come in many forms - biological women, adoptive women, foster women, and others who step into the role of a mother. Each of these forms of womanhood is celebrated and honored in this book.

This book aims to inspire and uplift. It commemorates the power and perseverance of women, highlighting their significant role in molding our world. It is hoped that readers will find in it a source of inspiration and a beacon of hope.

In writing this book, the intention was not to idealize or idolize any individual but to highlight the qualities that make women symbols of womanhood. Any perceived flaws or shortcomings are not ignored, but they are not the focus of this book. The focus is on the positive qualities that inspire and motivate.

One of the most profound insights this book offers is the enduring nature of the bonds we form when we impact the lives of others. Those we guide and nurture, those whose lives we touch, remain with us in spirit. They do not leave us or go away. They become part of our journey, our story, and the legacy we leave behind.

In conclusion, "And She Arose as a Mother" is an ode to Presidential Nominee Kamala Harris and women everywhere, using their journey as a guiding light. It is a testament to the power of womanhood and a tribute to the women who shape our world. It is hoped to inspire, uplift, and celebrate women in all their diverse forms. It is an apologia for the book, a defense of its purpose and intentions, and a celebration of its subject - the power and beauty of womanhood. As women, we are all part of this narrative, and our shared responsibility is to continue to rise and uplift others along the way.

Mrs. Hannah Acquah-Sampson
*Deputy Commissioner (Retired)*
*Ghana Revenue Authority (GRA)*

# Preface

Within the rich fabric of life, certain moments transcend the ordinary, transforming into pivotal landmarks that define our journey and influence the world we live in. This book, *"She Arose As A Mother,"* is a tribute to one such pivotal moment, a moment that took root on an ordinary day on September 6th, 2018. That was the day I first witnessed Presidential Nominee Kamala Harris, then a Democratic Senator from California, during the Judiciary confirmation hearings for a Supreme Court nominee on the Cable News Network ( CNN).

Her tenacity, unwavering pursuit of justice, and ability to maintain composure under intense scrutiny were truly inspiring. Even when faced with an evasive person, she upheld respect, addressing them as Sir or Madam, a reflection of her character. From that day on, my respect for Senator Harris only grew. It was not just her tenacity that drew me in, but her relentless commitment to action, the ceaseless action of the highest order.

Fast forward to May 1st, 2019, I found myself engrossed in the congressional hearing on the findings of Mueller's report on Russian interference in the 2016 election. Once again, then-Senator Harris stole the spotlight when she challenged an Attorney General during their exchange. The special counsel had penned a comprehensive report citing numerous instances that hinted at obstruction attempts. Some of these involved requests to the White House counsel to deceive investigators, which seemingly would have been carried out if staffers had not refused. As I watched her during a judicial hearing, I accorded her a place of honor.

As I juxtaposed the exchanges during both the hearings of the Supreme Court nominee and the Attorney General, I began to appreciate an

African which says, "There are ranks in the king's umbrella." It dawned on me that then-Senator Kamala Harris stands above many. I pictured Senator Harris with the vigor she fights for victims, and I could not gauge the amount of energy she would muster to fight her own daughter's predator. I could only envision her like a lioness charging after him and striking him down. She would have bared her arms, disregarding all measures of defense and scorning the predator. I deeply admire the selfless, unbiased concern that then-Senator Harris has for issues related to people's well-being, especially the vulnerable. Yet, there is a humble side about her that I am sure may often go unnoticed. Even when she realizes that a litigant is evasive, though pressing assertively, she speaks respectfully and reverently and addresses them as Sir or Madam.

I looked at her and saw a woman wrapped in a flowery language that an ordinary observer could discover. I was certain that she could be a perfect advocate for many more than she was doing. However, there were significant facts that I had stored up in my memory about previous elections. So, I settled that neither she nor any woman would be elected as an American President.

The ABC's The VIEW announced in the week of January 2019 that then-Senator Kamala would appear on the show to promote her memoir The Truths We Hold: An American Journey. I marked my calendar, and lo and behold, on Tuesday, January 8th, 2019, she appeared. After exchanging pleasantries, she resumed her seat and then followed a series of questions. When asked if she was running for president, then Senator Harris responded, "So, I am pleased to announce to The View that I am not ready to make my announcement yet." As soon as Presidential Nominee Kamala Harris said that, they burst into laughter; they most expected her to say yes. It was now a reckoning moment to tell the world if she would run for the president of the great nation and "Why not?". Yet when she declined, I must say that my countenance had dropped. It felt like I had lost a treasure in the dust.

Nevertheless, on Monday, January 21st , 2019, on Martin Luther King's holiday, the then-California Senator Kamala Harris joined a crowded successional field of Democrats seeking to challenge the incumbent President. So, on Good Morning America, the then-Semar Harris announced that she would run for president in 2020. Less than a fortnight ago, she said she was not yet ready to announce a possible campaign, but here we are. At her announcement, my gracious heart rose into adoration of the Senator. Apparently, those who are good at blessing wit and truthfulness were quick at blessing God. Following the announcement, Senator Harris added, "I love my country. I love my country. This is a moment in time that I feel a sense of responsibility to stand up and fight for the best of who we are." The Senator added, "My entire career, as you mentioned, has been in keeping people safe. It is probably one thing that motivates me more than anything else. And when I look at this moment in time, I know the American people deserve somebody who's going to fight for them. Who's going to see them, who'll hear them, who will care about them, who will be concerned about their experience and put them in front of self-interest." What inspired me to write this book is when she mentioned that she grew up hearing America's beliefs. She said, "Our country was founded on noble ideals; we are the best of who we are when we fight to achieve those ideals. The thing about Dr. King that always inspires me is that he was aspirational. He was aspirational, like our country is aspirational. We know that we've not yet reached those ideals. But our strength is that we fight to reach those ideals".

I never missed watching the then-Senator Harris on the campaign trail. There was so much hope in her words, for they were very enthusiastic. They went on wheels, and the axles of the wheels were hot with speed: "Kamala for the people." Her utterances were earnest; they were hearty, very enthusiastic, and from a former prosecutor, a woman of pens and ink, a fierce yet loving letter woman. To see her on fire on the campaign trail was something very remarkable.

Motivated by her resilience and leadership, I was inspired to pen a book about her. However, my vision of her was not limited to her potential as our nation's president. I saw her as a multifaceted figure - a mother to her children, an aunt to her nieces and nephews, a sister to her siblings, a grandmother to her grandchildren, and a friend to those she cherishes, making her a unique leader in the global arena.

Despite being vociferous and determined to lead her party to the polls, the news many, like myself, did not want was came. On Tuesday, December 3rd, 2019, then-Senator Harris abruptly released a video on Twitter to end her 2020 presidential campaign. "To you, my supporters, my dear supporters, it is with deep regret — but also with deep gratitude — that I am suspending our campaign today. But I want to be clear with you: I am still very much in this fight," Harris continued. "And I will keep fighting every day for what this campaign has been about Justice for the people, All the people."

The video, without a doubt, was a sorrowful lament, as my eye rests on her many campaign trails, but without any evidence, it felt like she would metamorphosis and appear in another form. I was hopeful, yet without anything to substantiate my hope.

Thus, the trajectory of events took an unforeseen turn. Her sudden withdrawal from the presidential race and subsequent acceptance of the vice-presidential role led me to pause my project. Despite this, I held onto a spark of hope, a belief that she might one day rise to the presidency.

With this hope at heart, I meticulously safeguarded the manuscript, treating it as a seed awaiting the right season to flourish. I believed in this book's potential to inspire, enlighten, and illuminate this extraordinary woman's journey. Though on hold, the manuscript was far from forgotten - it was a pledge of a story yet to be fully narrated, a tale that could one day unfold with her ascent to the presidency. This book is a tribute to her journey, a celebration of her spirit, and a testament to her achievements. It is a story of discovery, of a journey that transcends the personal and becomes a testament to a collective struggle and victory.

This book, while primarily a tribute to the Democratic Presidential Nominee Kamala Harris, it is also a celebration of every woman who has dared to dream, fight, and rise. It is an homage to the mothers in every nation who rise to champion justice, equality, and a brighter future for their children.

This book serves as a beacon, casting a guiding light on the path of those who dare to dream and strive for a better world. It stands as a testament to the indomitable spirit of women everywhere, their resilience, courage, and unwavering commitment to justice and equality.

As we journey through this book, let's reflect on the concept of Divine Providence. When the wheel of Providence spins rapidly, we can only see the outer circle. But if we look back at history and read the story of a thousand years, we see one overarching theme - that God is working out His everlasting purposes in the world. We see that one event counteracts another. If we reflect on our life, not just today, but look back on decades of it, we will find ourselves blessing God for His Providence amongst us.

About 35 years ago, Gerald Ford, the former U.S. President, had a unique opportunity to visit the Herbert Hoover Presidential Library and Museum in West Branch, Iowa. This visit happened on October 18th , 1989, nearly a decade after his presidency had concluded. This event gave him a special platform to educate the younger generation about the important roles that ex-presidents continue to play in American society, even after their term in office.

In this setting, he was relieved from the need to evade the incisive questions journalists often ask. Instead, a young girl asked him, "What advice would you give to a young lady who aspires to be the president of the United States?" Responding with an optimistic smile, the ex-president said, "Well, I do hope that at some point, we will see a young lady become the president of the United States."

Ford further added, "I can tell you how I think it will happen because it won't follow the typical course of events."

Remember, every journey begins with a single step. Every dream, no matter how grand, starts with a simple thought. Every fight, no matter how daunting, begins with a single act of defiance. And every rise, no matter how steep, starts from the ground. So dare to dream, dare to fight, and dare to rise. The world needs more dreamers, more fighters, and more risers. Who knows? The next dreamer, fighter, or riser could be you. As the wheel of Providence continues to turn, I pray that we see nothing but a cycle of everlasting wisdom.

Presidential Nominee  Harris is a wonderfully respectable, adorable, and generous woman, a gift to America's federal republic. I have often wondered why scarcely anybody had much to say about her. Yet, as you delve into this book, remember that it is not just a story about Presidential Nominee Kamala Harris. It is a story about you, about us, about every woman who has ever dared to dream, to fight, and to rise. It is a story of hope, resilience, and the power of the human spirit. Above all, it is a story of how we can all rise to become mothers in our nations in the face of adversity.

May this book remind you of that journey, a guiding light leading you on your own path of discovery. May it inspire you to dream, fight, and rise, just as Presidential Nominee  Kamala Harris and countless women have done before.

May this book inspire you as the journey of  Presidential Nominee Kamala Harris inspired me. Today, as we stand on the brink of a new era, let's remember that every moment, every struggle, and every triumph has led us to where we are now. And in God's perfect timing,

we are exactly where we are meant to be. This is the culmination of our journey, which has led us to this moment, this place, and this understanding of the world and our place in it. May this book serve as a reminder of that journey, and may it inspire you to embark on your own journey of discovery.

President Gerald Ford's prediction and numerous other instances that we are witnessing after 35 years serve as a testament to the exceptional circumstances that often lay the groundwork for revolutionary change. It reaffirms the existence of a voice in Providence, which might go unheard if we are too absorbed in misogyny, hatred, racism, and the like.

There are also the voices of the nation's founding fathers, which frequently communicate with us but often go unheard as they protest against our inhumanity. There is a voice in God's Providence as well. He communicates so much to His children and flocks through every stroke of His rod and every blessing of His daily Providence.

There is a voice emanating from President Gerald Ford's grave — a message in every woman's voice speaking to those who are willing to listen, that America is more than ready for a female president, such as Presidential Nominee Kamala Harris.

Welcome to "Until I Arose as a Mother in My Nation."

# Prelude

A figure of resilience and strength emerges in the vibrant and ever-evolving landscape of American politics. The Democratic Presidential Nominee Kamala Harris stands tall. She is a symbol of motherly love and unwavering dedication. Her journey, a powerful narrative of a woman who rose to the highest echelons of power, inspires all.

This book is not just about Presidential Nominee Kamala's political ascent but also a tribute to all mothers. Mothers by birth, mothers by adoption, foster mothers, and those who step into the role of a mother, offering their love, guidance, and support to those who need it. It celebrates motherhood in all its forms and its profound impact on shaping our world.

Presidential Nominee Kamala Harris herself is a testament to this power of motherhood. Her motherly instincts have guided her decisions, shaped her leadership style, and influenced her governance approach. Her rise to power was not without challenges, but like a true mother, she faced them head-on, protecting and nurturing her country's dreams and aspirations. Her loyalty to her nation and its people is unwavering, just like a mother's loyalty to her children.

This book invites you to explore Presidential Nominee Kamala's life, career, and role as a mother in America. It is a celebration of a remarkable woman who leaves an indelible mark on history with every step she takes.

So, let us embark on this journey, guided by the light of Presidential Nominee Kamala's loyalty and motherly love. Let us learn from her experiences, draw inspiration from her wisdom, and find a beacon

of hope and a model of resilience in her story. For in the annals of history,  Presidential Nominee Kamala Harris' name will forever be associated with the power of loyalty, the choice to do right, and the courage to forge ahead. This is the story of  Presidential Nominee Kamala, the guiding light, the mother who arose.

And as we delve into this story, let us also take a moment to honor all mothers. Those who have nurtured, guided, and helped us become who we are. Mothers, in all their forms, are our society's pillars, the future's architects, and the unsung heroes of our everyday lives. Their love, their sacrifice, and their unwavering belief in us are what make us rise. So here's to all mothers and to Presidential Kamala Harris, a mother who arose to lead a nation. May her story inspire us, her love guides us, and her strength empowers us. This is the Democratic Presidential Nominee Kamala  Harris and every woman's ode, their tribute, their song. "And she arose as a mother".

# Apologia

This book, "And She Arose as a Mother," is a tribute to the power of motherhood, as embodied by the Democratic Presidential Nominee Kamala Harris, and by extension, all mothers. It is not intended to be a political commentary or an endorsement of any particular political ideology. Rather, it is an exploration of the qualities of motherhood - love, sacrifice, resilience, and loyalty - that are universally admired and respected.

The book draws on the public life and career of Presidential Nominee Kamala Harris as a source of inspiration, but it is not a biography. It does not delve into her personal life or make judgments about her private decisions. Instead, it focuses on her public persona and her role as a mother figure in American politics.

The book also acknowledges the diversity of motherhood. It recognizes that mothers come in many forms - biological mothers, adoptive mothers, foster mothers, and others who step into the role of a mother. Each of these forms of motherhood is celebrated and honored in this book.

I aim for this book to inspire and uplift. The book is a celebration of the strength and resilience of mothers and a testament to their profound impact on shaping our world. It is hoped that readers will find in it a source of inspiration and a beacon of hope.

In writing this book, the intention was not to idealize or idolize Presidential Nominee Kamala Harris but to highlight the qualities that make her a symbol of motherhood. Any perceived flaws or shortcomings are not ignored, but they are not the focus of this book. The focus is on the positive qualities that inspire and motivate.

In conclusion, "And She Arose as a Mother" is an ode to mothers everywhere, using the journey of Presidential Nominee Kamala Harris as a guiding light. It is a testament to the power of motherhood and a tribute to the women who shape our world. The book is hoped to inspire, uplift, and celebrate mothers in all their diverse forms. It is an apologia for the book, a defense of its purpose and intentions, and a celebration of its subject - the power and beauty of motherhood.

# Kamala

## *A Testament to Grace and Resilience*

This chapter delves into the inspiring journey of Vice President and Presidential Nominee Kamala Harris, a figure of grace and resilience. It explores her rise, fueled by a mother's love and grace, and her unwavering faith in divine sufficiency. The narrative further illuminates her voyage in God's grace, her testament of faith and divine strength, and her journey of grace upon grace. The chapter also highlights her role as an advocate for the voiceless, a voice of the people, a prosecutor of prowess, an ascending attorney, a guardian of justice, and a mother on the side of truth. Through her story, we witness a journey marked by grace, resilience, and an unwavering commitment to justice and truth.

# Kamala's Rise:
## *A Mother's Love and Grace*

In wisdom's world, love, grace do abound,
Momala, our Kamala, her rise is profound.
Her journey, testament to a mother's grace,
A beacon of love, shining in every place.

No need to envy, grace appeared gloriously,
And the appearance is abiding, daily.
Kamala, grace symbol, among us stands,
Her spirit of grace, reaching out hands.

Her grace, not fleeting like a man,
But abiding with us, a mother's plan.
Her words of grace, a prayer for all,
Echoing in spirits, answering the call.

Not hollow words, but the fairest light,
Kamala's words, a mother's wisdom, bright.
Her grace, like precious pearls, spread wide,
In every heart, her love, grace reside.

Then shall our meditations be sweet,
Blessed with Kamala's grace, love our creed.
In life's tapestry, Kamala, our beloved mother,
Her rise to the top, a journey of grace.

Kamala's grace, a river that flows,
Doug, her husband, in awe of her glow.
Radiant, Kamala, a mother, shines in grace,
Despite life's trials, she sets the pace.

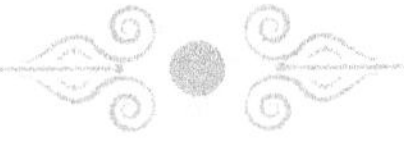

# Kamala:
## *A Mother's Trust in Divine Sufficiency*

Kamala, a mother, stands with faith,
In God's sufficiency, she finds her wraith.
"Our sufficiency is of God," she proclaims,
In His wisdom and love, she aims.

In the political realm, her wisdom shines,
Guiding her children, through tough times.
With God's love, she leads the way,
In her heart, His teachings stay.

She nurtures the nation, with love and care,
Her actions speak, beyond compare.
In the face of adversity, she stands tall,
With God's sufficiency, she conquers all.

Her journey continues, with steadfast pace,
Serving the nation, with grace.
Kamala, a mother, her story unfolds,
A testament to God's love, it holds.

Kamala, the mother, her trust unwavering,
In Divine sufficiency, her faith anchoring.
With each step taken, each challenge faced,
She leads with love, with God's grace.

Kamala's assurance, a beacon of hope,
Helping the nation, with challenges to cope.
With God's love, her guiding light,
She serves the nation, with all her might.

# Kamala's Journey:
## *A Mother's Voyage in God's Grace*

In the sea of politics, Kamala sails,
Her sufficiency in God, never fails.
Like a child traveling with a father,
She draws from His love, like no other.

In the vast ocean of governance, she steers,
Guided by God's love, she perseveres.
With every wave, every tide,
In God's sufficiency, she takes pride.

She navigates the challenges, with ease,
Her faith in God, her heart's keys.
In the voyage of service, she finds joy,
Her love for her children, her buoy.

Her journey is long, the sea is vast,
But with God's grace, she's steadfast.
Kamala, a mother, sails through the night,
In the voyage of politics, she's a guiding light.

Kamala, the mother, in God's grace,
Her love for nation, like an embrace.
With each word spoken, each action taken,
She shapes the nation, its core unshaken.

Kamala, the mother, her journey's not done,
For the quest for justice is never won.
With each new dawn, she rises again,
A testament to resilience, in the face of pain.

# Kamala's Journey:
## *A Testament Of Faith And Divine Strength*

In the journey of life, where challenges abound,
Kamala, our Momala, her faith profound.
Her strength, not of her own, but divine,
From God All-sufficient, forever to shine.

Kamala called her pastor, voice clear and strong,
"Pray for me, Doug, and this country's throng.
For the race I'm intending to run,
May God's will in all be done."

Kamala's confidence leans upon God alone,
Almighty, All-sufficient, on His divine throne.
Kamala's faith hangs upon God, so true,
In His all-sufficiency, she cannot rue.

The Lord, all-sufficient in power and love,
Guides Kamala through life, from His throne above.
Through mazes and trials, He finds a way,
In His all-sufficient love, Kamala sways.

God, the All-sufficient, Kamala's strength, her song,
In His love and mercy, she belongs.
Kamala, our Momala, in God's grace,
Runs the race, at her own pace.

In the tapestry of life, Kamala, strong and brave,
Her faith in God, her soul to save.
Her rise to the top, a journey of faith,
In God's All-sufficient love, she bathes.

# Kamala:
## *A Journey of Grace Upon Grace*

In the voice of Mary, blessed by grace,
I, Kamala, find my place.
From humble beginnings, my journey begins,
A tale of resilience, as time spins.

"By the grace of God, I am what I am,"
This is my confession, so grand.
In the halls of justice, I found my home,
Among the laws, no longer alone.

From a prosecutor to attorney general,
My path was anything but conventional.
Each step a testament to grace,
In the grand tapestry of life, I traced.

To senator, then vice president,
Each role a significant testament.
The grace that quickened me, set me free,
From the chains of doubt, it's my decree.

Now, a presidential nominee,
My journey has been a testimony.
The smallest pearl, the brightest gem,
Each reflects the grace bestowed on them.

So here I stand, with stories to tell,
Of victories won and times I fell.
Yet through it all, one truth remains,
"By the grace of God," my spirit gains.

And now, as I continue on my way,
Each step I take, each word I say,

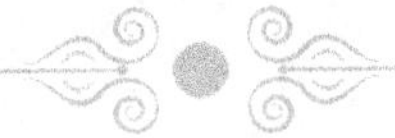

Reflects my journey, grace upon grace,
A testament to unmeritted grace on me.

THIS PAGE INTENTIONALLY LEFT BLANK

# Kamala

## *The Voice of Justice and Truth*

This chapter explores Vice President and Presidential Nominee Kamala Harris's role as an advocate for the voiceless, a voice of the people, a prosecutor of prowess, an ascending attorney, a guardian of justice, and a mother on the side of truth. It delves into her unwavering commitment to justice and her relentless pursuit of truth. The narrative illuminates her courage in the face of adversity, her resilience in the pursuit of justice, and her integrity in the realm of politics. Through her story, we witness a journey marked by strength, resilience, and an unwavering commitment to truth and justice. This chapter serves as a testament to Vice President and Presidential Nominee Kamala Harris's indomitable spirit and her relentless pursuit of justice for all.

# Kamala:
## *The Advocate of the Voiceless*

In the theater of justice, Kamala takes the stage,
A beacon of hope, breaking every cage.
As a prosecutor, she's been the voice of the unheard,
In the symphony of law, she's the resonating word.

"Has she not fought for the oppressed and the weak?
Why not for us, should we seek?"
The victims of crime, the marginalized in sight,
See in her a warrior, a beacon of light.

The victim of injustice says, "She's fought for one like me,
If I could but emulate her, I too could be free."
The voiceless exclaims, "She's advocated for those in plight,
If I could but follow her, I'd find my right."

They're not sure they can match her, yet they believe,
For they've seen her victories, ready to achieve.
She's shown her power, her will to redress,
In her, they see a path to progress.

Oh, that all would see this truth so clear,
As plain as a theorem, as dear.
She's achieved much, so why not me?
To strive like her is as natural as can be.

Just as one eats when hunger calls,
Or drinks when thirst befalls,
So should one strive like Kamala's pace,
And in her inspiring journey, find their place.

For she's done great deeds, shown love and grace,
Akin to the blessings from above, she's left a trace.

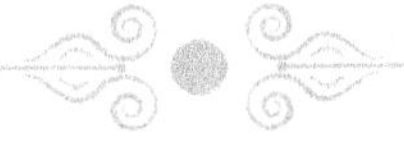

So let us come to her, let us begin,
And like a great multitude, in her footsteps we'll spin.

# Kamala:
## *The Voice of the People*

She stands in the center, strong and true,
Speaking for the many, not just the few.
Not a sacrifice to popular fury,
But a testament to a future, bright and worry-free.

Kamala, a beacon of hope, shining so bright,
Guiding us through, even the darkest night.
Her voice, a melody, resonating far and wide,
A symbol of strength, in whom we confide.

She walks with grace, her head held high,
Underneath the vast, infinite sky.
Her words, like a river, flowing free,
Painting a picture of what the world could be.

In the face of adversity, she stands tall,
A testament to the fact, that love conquers all.
Her spirit, unbroken, like the mighty sea,
Kamala, the voice of the people, forever she'll be.

Kamala, not just a leader, but a mother so dear,
Nurturing us, wiping away every tear.
With a heart full of love, and hands so kind,
She's a solace, a comfort, for every troubled mind.

Her wisdom, like a lighthouse, guiding us through,
Showing us the path, honest and true.
With every word, every action, every deed,
She sows in our hearts, a hopeful seed.

Kamala, the voice of the people, loud and clear,
A voice of courage, that we all hold dear.
With her at the helm, we have nothing to fear,
For a brighter future is finally here.

# Kamala:
## *The Prosecutor's Prowess*

In the courtrooms of justice, Kamala stands tall,
A prosecutor of power, answering the call.
Her voice, a beacon, cutting through the unheard,
In the symphony of law, she's the resonating word.

"Has she not fought for the oppressed and the weak?
Why not for us, should we seek?"
The victims of crime, the marginalized in sight,
See in her a warrior, a beacon of light.

The victim of injustice says, "She's fought for one like me,
If I could but emulate her, I too could be free."
The voiceless exclaims, "She's advocated for those in plight,
If I could but follow her, I'd find my right."

They're not sure they can match her, yet they believe,
For they've seen her victories, ready to achieve.
She's shown her power, her will to redress,
In her, they see a path to progress.

In the heart of the nation, Kamala's story unfolds,
A tale of resilience, as each chapter beholds.
Her journey inspires, her victories ignite,

A beacon for all, shining ever so bright.
So, they say, "If we could, we too would stand tall,
Fight for justice, answer the call.
With Kamala as our mother,
We too will strive, no matter how far."

# Kamala:
## *The Attorney's Ascent*

In the legal cosmos, Kamala ascends,
An attorney, on whom justice depends.
Her path, a beacon in the legal fray,
Guiding those lost along the way.

"Could we not follow where she dares to tread?
Could we not seek justice, as she has led?"
Those lost in the labyrinth of law,
See in her a compass, a trusted confide.

One entangled in justice's maze wonders aloud,
"Could I find freedom, as she has?"
Wandering soul proclaims, "Could I find my way,
If I follow her light, in the night?"

And now they declare, "Could we not also rise,
Fight for justice, answer the call?
With Kamala as our guiding star,
Could we not strive, no matter how far?"

In the realm of law, Kamala's ascent is clear,
Her victories echo, far and near.
Her journey, a testament to her might,
A beacon for all, shining ever so bright.

So here's to Kamala, the attorney, the guide,
In her wisdom and courage, we take pride.
A symbol of justice, a beacon of change,
In the annals of law, her name will remain.

# Kamala:
## *The Guardian of Justice*

Kamala, the nation's mother, guards justice, steady hand,
Ensures fairness, her love blankets the land.
Not swayed by power, nor by might,
Guided by what's just, and what's right.

In disaster's face, Kamala stands tall,
A beacon of hope for one and all.
Her courage unwavering, her spirit bright,
A guiding star in the darkest night.

Kamala hears mutiny whisper in hushed tones,
Quells the unrest, soothes the groans.
For in her heart, she knows it's true,
Justice prevails, and will break through.

Kamala walks the path few have tread,
With the weight of justice overhead.
Yet, she carries it with grace and ease,
She is Kamala, the guardian of peace.

In the end, when all is done,
Kamala stands victorious, the battle won.
For she is Kamala, strong and free,
The Guardian of Justice, for all to see.

Kamala, the guardian, her journey's not done,
For justice's fight is never won.
With each new dawn, she rises again,
A testament to resilience, in the face of pain.

# Kamala:
## *A Mother on the Side Of Truth:*

In a world where power is a game,
And truth is often not the aim.
Where untruthful people evolve,
Acting untruthfully, their integrity dissolves.

They are not honest, not even commonly so,
Towards those whose necessities generally plead for woe.
"They judge not the cause, the cause of the marginalized,
And the right of the needy, they do not recognize."

When a person becomes a rogue, all is fair game,
They'd rob the marginalized without any shame.
In this political world, stands Kamala, a mother on truth's side,
A contemporary leader, the digital age's guide.

Ignoring the crowd's scornful tweets,
Holding truth, a rose among cheats.
Unswayed by media lions, lobbyist's might,
Her armor, integrity; her weapon, light.

Facing fake news, she stands tall,
Her voice, a courageous call.
"I won't bow to falsehood's chain,
I am Kamala, mother on truth's side, I remain."

Walking her path under the scrutinizing sun,
A testament to courage, when all's done.
In life's amphitheater, many hide,
She stands open, truth as her guide.

Not in the crowd, but opinion's den,
Showing us what it means to live, then.
Here's to Kamala, may her spirit tire not,
In adversity's face, may her truth rot not.

In the realm of political twilight,
Kamala shines, a star so bright.
Her light pierces through the darkest night,
Guiding us towards what is right.
In this world of shadows and deceit,
Kamala stands strong, never admitting defeat.

# Kamala

## The Resilient Path of Progress

This chapter chronicles Vice President and Presidential Nominee Kamala Harris's journey through the political landscape, highlighting her readiness, resilience, and unwavering commitment to progress. It explores her tenacious preparedness, her ability to withstand the political furnace, and her steadfast loyalty. The narrative further illuminates her ascent as a mother in the political realm, her testament to political motherhood, and her attractive arc of achievement. The chapter also underscores her role as an advocate for the voiceless and a voice of the people. Through her story, we witness a journey marked by strength, resilience, and an unwavering commitment to justice and truth. This chapter serves as a testament to Vice President and Presidential Nominee Kamala Harris's indomitable spirit and her relentless pursuit of justice for all.

# Kamala:
## *Penning the Path of Progress*

In the quiet of the night, with pen in hand,
I write my story, across this great land.
From the halls of Howard, to the courts of law,
I've fought for justice, without a flaw.

I remember the day, clear as can be,
When Joe Biden called, and said to me,
"Kamala, my friend, will you stand by my side,
As we journey together, on this wild ride?"

Tears welled up, as I put down my pen,
Overwhelmed by the love, that I felt then.
Unworthy of the honor, yet called to serve,
I knew in my heart, I had the nerve.

The first of many, a path I pave,
For all the women, brave and brave.
A new era dawns, with a mother's care,
A testament to love, and a world that's fair.

From prosecuting cases, in the city by the bay,
To serving as senator, in a powerful way.
Every step I took, every path I tread,
Led me to this moment, as I forge ahead.

The first woman, the first of my race,
To hold this office, at such a pace.
A beacon of hope, a symbol of change,
In a world that's diverse, and beautifully strange.

My mother once told me, in her gentle way,
"You may be the first, but not the last, I pray."

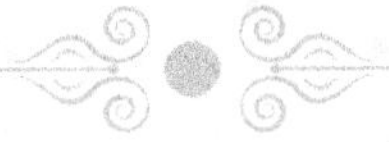

So I carry this torch, with pride and grace,
For all the women, who will take my place.


My story is one, of many a stride,
Of triumphs and trials, and taking pride.
In serving my country, in doing what's right,
In standing up for justice, with all my might.

So here I am, a mother in power,
Blooming brightly, like a sunflower.
The first of many, but certainly not the last,
Writing my story, honoring my past.

# Kamala:
## The Tapestry of Tenacious Preparedness

In the annals of history, a name does resound,
Of a king called Ethelred, the Unready was found.
Ineffectual ruler, his reign was fraught,
With battles lost, and wars he fought.

Yet in the modern age, a new tale unfurls,
Of a woman ready, to change the world.
Her name is Kamala, strong and steady,
Unlike Ethelred, she is always ready.

"Ready to work," she proudly proclaims,
In the halls of power, she stakes her claims.
From the streets of Oakland, to the Senate's grand halls,
She's ready to answer, whenever duty calls.

From Howard University, to the courts of law,
She's always ready, to give her all.
When Biden called, she didn't hesitate,
Ready to serve, to make America great.

Through trials and triumphs, she held her head high,
Ready to reach, for the limitless sky.
From prosecutor to senator, then vice president,
Her readiness, always evident.

In the face of adversity, she stands tall,
Ready to catch, those who fall.
A beacon of hope, in times of despair,
Ready to show, how much she cares.

So here's to Kamala, the Ready, the True,
A woman of power, breaking through.
Ready to lead, ready to fight,
Ready to guide America, towards the light.

# Kamala's Testament:
## *Through the Political Furnace*

In frailty, strength, I, Kamala, rise,
Chosen by God, not a surprise.
In politics' furnace heat, I stand,
Guided by love's divine command.

Beauty marred, character tried, in this trial,
False accusations, propaganda's vile.
Chosen as afflicted, not prosperous,
In pain, I trust, in God, focus.

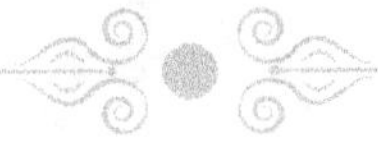

I choose the Lord, my mystery,
His choice of me, my history.
In politics' furnace, seven times hot,
I am not afraid, God forgets me not.

Strength melted, glory consumed, faith bloomed,
In glowing coals, grace is assumed.
His chosen, in politics' furnace, love glows,
In my frailty, I seek to improve, love shows.

Here I stand, Kamala, frail yet tall,
Chosen by God, to heed His call.
In politics' furnace, I find my worth,
Chosen for hearth, not palace's mirth.

In affliction, I am tried, tested, invested,
In God's love, I find rest, bested.
In politics' furnace, my faith refined, promise find,
In heat, God's hand, my life aligned.

In politics' furnace, I am not alone,
In heat, dread gone, His way shown.
Frail, human, yet divinely planned,
In politics' furnace, I find my way, love's hand.

In politics' furnace, beauty reborn, hope drawn,
In my frailty, I find strength, love's dawn.
In politics' furnace, my life aligned,
In my frailty, I grow, in His love, bind.

So, I, Kamala, in frailty stand, chosen,
By God's loving hand, love woven.
In politics' furnace, I find my worth,
Chosen for hearth, not for earth.

In my frailty, I seek to rise, my prize,
In His love, I realize.
In politics' furnace, seven times hot,
I fear not, God forgets me not.

# Kamala:
## *The Ready and Resilient*

In the annals of time, a tale is spun,
Of Ethelred the Unready, a king undone.
His rule was marked by strife and dread,
A reign of chaos, as his people bled.

Yet in our time, a new tale begins,
Of a woman ready, who knows no sins.
Her name is Kamala, her spirit, steady,
Unlike Ethelred, she is always ready.

"Ready to work," she boldly declares,
With every challenge, she bravely dares.
From the halls of Howard, to the Senate's grand halls,
She's ready to answer, whenever duty calls.

When Biden called, she did not falter,
Ready to serve, she did not alter.
From prosecutor to senator, then vice president,
Her readiness, always evident.

In the face of adversity, she stands tall,
Ready to catch, those who fall.

A beacon of hope, in times of despair,
Ready to show, how much she cares.

So here's to Kamala, the Ready, the True,
A woman of power, breaking through.
Ready to lead, ready to fight,
Ready to guide America, towards the light.

# Kamala:
## *The Ready and Steady*

In every endeavor, Kamala is ready to soar,
Ready to face, what's in store.
From student voters, to intellectual elites,
She's always ready, never admits defeat.

When tragedy struck, she was ready to console,
Compassion and empathy, playing a vital role.
In the lion's den, she's ready to roar,
Ready to face, what's in store.

So here's to Kamala, the Ready, the Brave,
A woman of power, who knows how to behave.
Ready to serve, ready to lead,
Ready to fulfill, America's need.

"I am ready to work," she proudly proclaims,
In the face of adversity, she never wanes.
From California to Washington, she's ready to serve,
Ready to give, the people deserve.

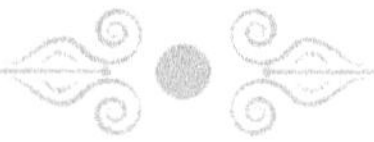

So here's to Kamala, the Ready, the Strong,
A woman of power, who's ready to belong.
Ready to lead, ready to inspire,
Ready to take, America higher.

# Kamala's Chronicle:
## A Mother's Ascent

In our nation's vast journey landscape,
Arose Kamala, a mother, vision preservative.
Observing her nation, in vast expanse,
Asked, "Who leads this great dance?"

Kamala, first woman Vice President, time's pioneer,
First South Asian descent woman, ascent sublime.
First African American descent woman, breaking mold,
First California Attorney General woman, bold.

She shattered glass ceilings, barriers dispelled,
Her titles, testament to battles quelled.
A testament to resilience, her determination,
A testament to journey, her narration.

Kamala, a mother by choice, deeds,
Her motherly compassion, like seed garden.
A guiding light indeed, in history annals,
"Who writes new chapter?" she echoes, channels.

In our nation's vast journey landscape,
Stands Kamala, ready for whatever comes.
The more she ponders, inquiry intensifies,

The more vibrant scenery, the wonderful story.

She knows she's qualified, has what it takes,
To lead her great nation, stakes.
With courage in heart, vision in sight,
Kamala steps forward, embracing the light.

Kamala, the mother, in her journey's ascent,
Her love for nation, her commitment.
With each step taken, each challenge faced,
She leads with love, with grace.

# Kamala's Journey:
## A Testament To Political Motherhood

In the political space, a woman of strength,
Kamala, a mother, her journey unfolds.
She bows humbly down, her words so clear,
"Not that I am capable of myself,"  she whispers.

A woman, inspired by God's grace, breaking limits,
Kamala, a force of nature, every minute.
Writing policies for nations, a task weighty,
Speaking with divine authority, voice so stately.

Her journey continues, her spirit never bends,
For she knows the journey matters more than ends.
With resilience and determination, she begins ascent,
Ready to lead, to serve, to represent.

In the grand theater of political endeavor, under sun,
Stands Kamala, ready for whatever may come.

For she knows she is capable, spirit unshakeable,
To lead her great nation, resolve unbreakable.

Kamala, the mother, in political sphere,
Her voice resonates, loud and clear.
With each word spoken, each action taken,
She shapes the nation, its core unshaken.

Kamala's journey, a testament to motherhood,
In political landscape, doing what she could.
Her love for her nation, deep and profound,
In her, a true leader is found.

# Kamala's Loyalty:
## *The Eye To Choose*

In grand tapestry of time, thread shines bright,
Kamala Harris, a beacon, radiating light.
Her journey, testament to loyalty's might,
In service of country, she takes flight.

Her position always new, challenges vast,
Yet stands undeterred by shadows cast.
With mantle of predecessors held fast,
She forges ahead, loyal to last.

In every relationship, loyalty is key,
In marriage, friendship, in unity.
Kamala embodies this, for all to see,
A loyal leader, as leaders should be.

Loyal to president, supporting his vision,
Loyal to nation, serving with precision.
Loyal to husband, in life's mission,
Loyal to friends, bond with no division.

She learns from those who came before,
Yet she is not them, so much more.
Her loyalty is not a chore,
But a choice, at its very core.

So here's to Kamala, loyal and true,
A guiding light for me and you.
In annals of history, her name will accrue,
A testament to loyalty, the eye to choose.

In heart of America, new dawn begins,
With Kamala, our beacon, where unity wins.
Her children jubilate, voices rise and fall,
In praise of Kamala, mother of all.

"Blessed, Blessed, Kamala," we sing with might,
Arise and lead us forward, guiding light.
In years to come, on solemn days, echo,
"May Kamala's influence continue to grow."

Guiding us with firm, yet gentle hand,
In grand tapestry of time, thread gleams,
Weaving a future, fabric of our dreams.

# Kamala:
## *The First Of Many*

In a world where firsts are often last,
A woman rose, shattering the glass.
Kamala, a name, now a beacon bright,
In the halls of power, she ignites the light.

A mother not by birth, but by deed,
To a nation's call, she paid heed.
Nurturing hope, justice, and truth,
Kamala, the mother of our youth.

She walks a path, both old and new,
In her steps, hope accrues.
A path paved by women of yore,
Kamala strides ahead, opening the door.

In the courtrooms, amidst the legal throng,
She found a place where she belongs.
A voice for the voiceless, she chose to be,
In pursuit of justice, equality, and liberty.

From the Golden State to the capital's dome,
She carried her fight, she made it known.
With every word, every law, every debate,
She weaves a story, a destiny, a fate.

So here's to Kamala, a force so bright,
May her journey continue, strong and right.
The first of many, she takes her stand,
In the annals of history, her name is grand.

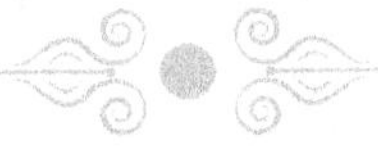

# Kamala:
## *The Attractive Arc of Achievement*

In the grand orchestra of life, Kamala's note rings true,
An attractive force, a vision anew.
Her resume, a sonnet of strength and light,
A torch held high in the darkest night.

Whispers of her deeds ripple through the land,
A beacon of hope, a future so grand.
From justice's chambers to the Senate's stage,
Her achievements are chapters on history's page.

A lawyer, a senator, a presidential journey,
In every challenge, she's emerged worthy.
A voice for the voiceless, a guardian of rights,
A star shining bright in political nights.

She healed the wounds of justice, made sight divine,
With every verdict, a truth to underline.
She lifted the hopes of those left behind,
In her, their dreams and aspirations intertwined.

Believe in her work, in her power to uplift,
A nation, a people, from the abyss adrift.
Trust in her wisdom, in her guiding hand,
For she has the vision to understand.

Her story flows, from coast to coast,
From the frosty North to the sunny South post.
A saga of triumph, of battles won,
Under her leadership, a new era begun.

So here's to Kamala, her attractive resume,
May her achievements light our way.

In the annals of history, her name is etched,
A testament to a journey, far from its stretch

# four

# Kamala

## *The Resilient Pursuit of Leadership*

This chapter chronicles Vice President and Presidential Nominee Kamala Harris's quest for earned nomination, her vision as a mother in the political realm, and her testament to resilience and determination. It explores her ascent in the face of challenges, her odyssey marked by resilience and leadership, and her position as America's choice. The narrative illuminates her unwavering commitment to serve the people, her readiness to face challenges, and her relentless pursuit of justice. Through her story, we witness a journey marked by strength, resilience, and an unwavering commitment to justice and truth.

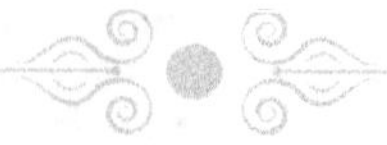

# Kamala's Quest:
## *The Pursuit Of Earned Nomination*

In life's grand arena of nomination,
Kamala stands, a beacon of strength.
Her spirit, resilience, unwavering faith,
Guides actions, determines her path.

Our Momala, Kamala, adds mystery,
To our nation's grand history.
Her story, journey, humble start,
Touches all, resonates in heart.

She stands with humble determination,
Not just endorsement, but proclamation.
Earning nomination is her aspiration,

Strives for validation in each action.
Like Esther, who became queen,
Trusted in unseen God, serene.
Kamala will do her part,
Trusts higher command, with heart.

Listens to people, understands plight,
Works for them, day and night.
Intends to earn place, actions clear,
Not about title, but respect dear.

Does not interfere, with divine providence,
Leaves events' course, in benign hands.
Waiting patiently, with confident repose,
In All-sufficient Lord, trust she bestows.

May we learn, her patient grace,
See Lord's glory, in every place.

All-sufficient Lord, will clear way,
Our souls shall know, joyous day.

Here's to Kamala, strong and true,
Her journey inspires, me and you.
In the end, it's not the crown,
But love and grace, that are renown.

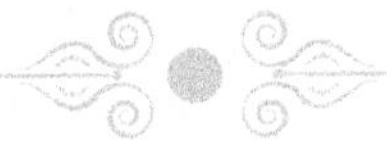

# Kamala's Quest:
## *A Mother's Vision*

In the political home, ideas are sown,
Stands Kamala, a mother, wisdom well-known.
Surveying her nation, in breadth and length,
She asked, "Who wields the political strength?"

"Who is versed in political discourse?" she muses,
As she gazes at stars, in quiet chooses.
Is it the one with power, riches, acclaim?
Or the one who can master political game?

"Perhaps," she thinks, "it's not about game, glory,
But serving people, telling their story.
It's not about power, wealth, fame,
But making a difference, the ultimate aim."

So, in the political home, ideas take flight,
Stands Kamala, a mother, embracing fight.
With a profound vision, heart full of grace,
She's ready to lead, in democratic space.

Kamala, the mother, in political sphere,
Her voice resonates, loud and clear.
With each word spoken, each action taken,
She shapes the nation, its core unshaken.

Kamala's quest continues, her vision unwavering,
In the political landscape, her influence towering.
With each step taken, each policy's formation,
She leads with love, caring for nation.

Kamala, the mother, her journey's not done,
For the quest for justice is never won.
With each new dawn, she rises again,
A testament to resilience, in the face of pain.

# Kamala's Ascent:
## *A Testament to Resilience and Determination*

In life's grand arena, challenges abound,
Stands Kamala, beacon of hope, strength found.
Kamala's spirit, resilience, unwavering faith,
Guides her actions, determines her path.

Against odds, Kamala rises, fearless,
She's human, but her spirit's limitless.
Kamala, limited in power, determination boundless,
Trust in her abilities, never wavering, soundless.

Kamala claims not to have all answers,
Nor alters course of events, no dancers.
She knows she's not here by chance,

As a servant, her work's wisely advanced.

She dares not be wiser than mentors,
For she's of their council, no pretenders.
Their strategies choice is wise, she believes,
Even when unconventional, she perceives.

Her limitations, of no consequence,
For her strength is in resilience.
Kamala shuns not duty for uncertainties,
That'd be a daring act, recklessness.

Kamala looks at challenges, fresh perspective,
No longer distressing her, or reflective.
But rather, she sees them as opportunities,
For her growth, development, communities.

Kamala listens no more to doubts,
Which whisper, "I am a woman."
But hears inner strength's voice,
In this, Kamala finds power, rejoice.

May Kamala's ode serve as tribute,
To all women who rise, contribute.
For in their journey, they inspire all,
To rise, to strive, to never fall.

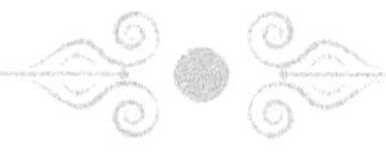

# Kamala's Odyssey:
## *A Testament of Resilience and Leadership*

In political endeavor's grand theater,
Stands Kamala, hope's beacon, strength's meter.
With a mother's heart, observing nation,
Asks, "Who's qualified to lead this creation?"

She sees mountains to climb, rivers cross,
Battles to fight, victories and loss.
Yet, she stands firm, resolve never sways,
Knows every challenge is but a phase.

"Who's qualified to lead this nation?" she ponders,
Looks at stars, in silence, wonders.
Is it the one with power, wealth, fame?
Or the one playing the political game?

No, she realizes, looking at dawn,
It's the one going when hope is gone.
The one who can inspire, understand, relate,
Sees a challenge not as curse, but fate.

So, she steps forward, spirit never bends,
Knows journey matters more than ends.
With resilience, determination, begins ascent,
Ready to lead, serve, represent.

In political endeavor's grand theater, under sun,
Stands Kamala, ready for whatever may come.
For she knows she's qualified, takes what it takes,
To lead her great nation, no matter the stakes.

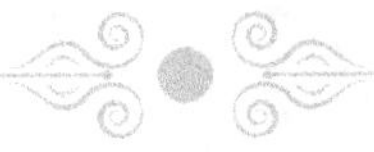

# Kamala:
## *America's Choice*

Kamala, chosen from the people, leads us true,
In her, we see our hopes renew.
No aristocrat, but a beacon bright,
Guiding us through the darkest night.

Born not to privilege, but to strive,
In her, the American Dream is alive.
From common roots, she rose high,
A testament to those who try.

Not just the elite's representative,
But a leader who is truly sensitive.
To the needs of all, she listens,
In her eyes, democracy glistens.

She walks the halls where power resides,
Yet, the people's voice inside her guides.
No gilded palace, but the streets,
Inform her policy and her feats.

She, too, knows struggle and sacrifice,
And it's this that gives her advice.
A wisdom born from life's reality,
Shapes her vision for equality.

In her journey, she's not alone,
With the people's trust, she has grown.
Their hopes and dreams, she carries,
A burden of love that never varies.

Kamala, America's choice, stands tall,
In her, we see the best of all.

A leader from the people, for the people,
On a journey that has no sequel.

# *five*

# Kamala

## *The Unwearied Athlete of Politics*

This chapter illuminates Vice President and Presidential Nominee Kamala Harris's unwearied journey in the political arena. It highlights her relentless pursuit of serving her nation, her unwavering energy, and her testament to resilience and leadership. Through her story, we witness a journey marked by strength, resilience, and an unwavering commitment to justice and truth. This chapter serves as a testament to Vice President and Presidential Nominee Kamala Harris's indomitable spirit and her relentless pursuit of justice for all. It highlights her dedication, her tireless efforts, and her unwavering commitment to her nation and its people. This chapter is a tribute to Vice President and Presidential Nominee Kamala Harris, the unwearied athlete, running the marathon of politics with grace, strength, and an unyielding spirit of service.

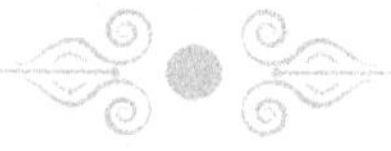

# Kamala:
## *The Unwearied Athlete*

In life's race, where men's pace sets beat,
Kamala runs, unwearied, meeting children's needs.
A race not often chosen by women,
For quiet pace with ability is aligned.

Yet Kamala, with overflowing strength, strides gracefully,
Not in wind's excess, but towards her place.
Her path, though right, isn't tread alone,
For zeal's incitements to her were shown.

Success has paces, some fast, some slow,
All who enter by faith, to end will go.
Like the snail into ark, some creep,
Chosen to succeed, they're safe, Kamala speaks.

No need to imitate slow, lame, weak,
Respect for their journey, ours shouldn't be meek.
Kamala walks with dignity, consistency her guide,
On success's path, where she strides.

Walking may be pace of many called,
But some, with touched hearts, have others enthralled.
These are mightiest, women of renown,
Like Samba-Panza, Thatcher, Kamala with crown.

Kamala, women's flower, under God, hope, strength,
Runs the race, not walks, to any length.
Light of foot as roes, swifter than eagles,
Stronger than lions, zealous for rights.

# Kamala:
## *Running At The Pace Of Energy*

In a world where many walk with a light foot,
Leaving no impression on life's sandy route,
Kamala runs, leaving footprints deep and clear,
Marks of resolve that echo in the ear.

Many touch life's nails with a dainty hand,
Afraid to hurt, they make no firm stand.
But Kamala, with hammer in grip, drives them in,
Her work is earnest, filled with a resonating din.

Some people's work, if it can be called so,
Leaves no sweat, no sign of a hearty blow.
But Kamala, she makes the iron hot by striking,
Seizes the present, for her, no time for biding.

With both hands, she works, the anvil rings,
Bound to fulfill her work with vigor that sings.
Service to her children, to God, her highest engagement,
Deserves nothing less than her full ennoblement.

All that is within Kamala blesses her kin,
Her spiritual faculties strained to the brim.
The service of her nation, her ultimate test,
Demands all her strength, her very best.

Running, then, as a mother, Kamala understands,
An energetic spiritual life, a life that expands.
She runs the race set before her with grace,
Her faith expecting success to embrace.

Every woman, every man, should strive to outdo,
The energy of their roles, to their purpose be true.

So Kamala runs in her Master's ways,
Proving that Her children can render Her praise.

# Kamala:
## *The Mother's Marathon of Warmth*

Running, a pace that warms the soul,
Kamala embraces this, her goal.
In the depth of winter's icy hold,
She runs, her spirit bold, her story told.

No fire of Christmas logs piled high,
Can warm Kamala as much as when she tries.
The comforts of the gospel, the doctrines of grace,
In Kamala's race, are magnified, take place.

Kamala stands, converted and true,
Not just a hearer, but a doer, through and through.
Others may demand comfort, grow selfish and unsure,
But Kamala finds joy in doing, her heart pure.

Kamala works for others, her heart's dedication,
Finds in this work, her own heart's elation.
In watering others, Kamala's soul is watered,
Her path, by the Good Physician, is chartered.

"Quicken your spiritual pace," He prescribes to Kamala,
"Throw more energy into the cause," He describes to Kamala.
And so, Kamala runs, her pace warming,
In the marathon of motherhood, her love storming.

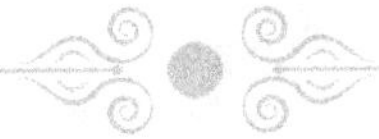

Kamala, the unwearied, her journey never ends,
Her love for her children, on no condition depends.
She runs, not for glory, not for fame,
But for love, in life's untamed game.

Her marathon continues, her spirit never tires,
Her love, like an eternal flame, never expires.
Kamala, the mother, running at the pace of warmth,
Leaves a legacy of love, of immeasurable worth.

# Kamala:
## The Mother's Marathon for America

Running, a pace that cheers the soul,
Kamala embraces this, her goal.
In the face of challenges, fears taking hold,
She runs for America, her spirit bold, her story told.

Running, the essence of her journey's start,
She shall not be weary, she plays her part.
Many start running, but soon they tire,
But Kamala runs on for America, her spirit never expires.

In the garden of life, many buds bloom,
But not all bear fruit, some meet their doom.
Yet Kamala, she waits upon America,
Her service to her nation, her ultimate era.

From the moment she's chosen, she serves not self,
But America, every hair, every part of herself.
Her business, to promote America's honor, America's glory,
This is Kamala's mission, her life's story.

If you do not belong to America in soul and heart,
You will grow weary, from its path you'll depart.
But Kamala, she is a consecrated servant of America,
She keeps up the running, to win the crown, she'll tread.

Kamala, the mother, runs for her children,
For every American, woman and men.
Her marathon continues, her spirit never tires,
Her love for America, like an eternal flame, never expires.

Kamala, the unwearied, her journey never ends,
Her love for America, on no condition depends.
She runs, not for glory, not for fame,
But for America, in life's untamed game.

# Kamala:
## *The Unfaltering Torchbearer*

Kamala, tireless in her stride, her journey knows no end,
Her love for America, unwavering, on no condition does it bend.
She runs, not for personal glory, not for fleeting fame,
But for America, in life's untamed, challenging game.

Kamala, the mother, runs for every child,
For every American, her efforts compiled.
Her marathon persists, her spirit never tires,
Her love for America, an eternal flame that inspires.

Running, a rhythm that fuels the soul,
Kamala embraces this, her ultimate goal.
In the marathon of life, weariness may take its toll,
But Kamala runs, her spirit whole, playing her role.

Kamala's solace, a promise so dear,
That she shall not be weary, this much is clear.
For decades on end, maybe more,
Kamala runs for America, her heart at the core.

How does Kamala run and not grow weary?
Because daily strength is given, her vision not bleary.
Not a stock of grace, but a constant stream,
Fuels Kamala's run, powers her dream.

As Kamala advances, fresh vistas catch her sight,
Like a traveler in awe of the scenery's might.
The towering mountains, the vast sea,
The mighty cliffs, the verdant fields, all set her free.

Wisdom, her guide, always a fresh source,
In its pages, Kamala finds her course.
The words of the wise, glowing with radiant glory,
Inspire Kamala's run, become part of her story.
So Kamala runs, and is not weary,
Her path lit by grace, her vision not bleary.
In the highway of righteousness, she finds her way,
Running for America, come what may.

Kamala, with her staff in hand,
Leads America, across the land.
Her pace steady, her resolve strong,
She runs for her children, all day long.

In the face of adversity, Kamala does not falter,
Her spirit, like the sea, does not alter.
She runs for justice, for truth, for right,
Kamala, the runner, is America's guiding light.

Running, Kamala carries the staff of hope,
With every challenge, she learns to cope.
Kamala, the runner, will not tire,
In the marathon of life, she continues to inspire.

# Kamala:
## *The Unwearied Torchbearer*

In the light of her purpose, Kamala strides,
A dedicated servant, by God's grace, she abides.
Her strength, a glory, from God, her guide,
In His service, she takes pride.

All strength, power, and intellect, Kamala receives,
From God, who in every form of existence, believes.
From the power of her arm, to the swiftness of her foot,
All strength is Kamala's, in her pursuit.

The keenness of her intellect, Kamala respects,
She, who has wrought wonders, projects.
To her unwavering hand, Kamala owes her fame,
Her physical strength, a testament to God's name.

The glory of Kamala's strength, a beacon for all,
It makes her vigorous, makes her stand tall.
So, Kamala gives the service of the strength God created,
To her nation, her life, her strength, is dedicated.

Kamala, the unwearied, her journey never ends,
Her love for her nation, on no condition depends.
She runs, not for glory, not for fame,
But for her nation, in life's untamed game.

# six

# Kamala

## *The Herald of Change*

In the vast expanse of political history, a new chapter unfolds with Vice President and Presidential Nominee Kamala Harris, a beacon of hope and change. Her journey, marked by resilience and determination, signifies a new era. As a leader, she stands not as a demi-god, but as a guide, illuminating the path towards justice and equality. This chapter delves into her inspiring journey, exploring how she has become a symbol of change and a role model for future generations.

# Kamala:
## *The Herald of Change*

Kamala, a beacon of hope in the twilight,
A leader emerging with strength and might.
She is not a demi god, not an idol, but a guide,
A force of change, with truth and justice by her side.

She heralds a change, a new dawn,
A chance to right what's been wrong.
Not bound by the chains of the past,
But free to create a peace that will last.

In the heart of the nation, she plants a seed,
A leader, not a demi god, is what we need.
She stands tall, in the political tide,
With truth and justice as her guide.

She speaks for those who've been unheard,
Transforms their cries into powerful words.
She fights for rights, for equality,
In her, we see a new reality.

No more demi gods, no more deceit,
With her leadership, the old retreat.
Under her watch, a new sun will rise,
A future of truth, with no disguise.

The old guard's demi gods, once held dear,
Are cast aside, they disappear.
"What have we  to do any more with demi gods?" we say,
For in our hearts, Kamala lights the way.

# Kamala:
## *The Path Paver*

In the land of the brave, the home of the free,
A woman stood tall, as tall as a tree.
Kamala, a name, a legacy, a dream,
In the river of time, she's a powerful stream.

Born of immigrants, in a land far and wide,
She took on the world, with hope as her guide.
A mother, a daughter, a sister, a wife,
She's played many roles in her vibrant life.

In the halls of justice, she made her mark,
Her voice resonating, strong and stark.
A path paver, a trailblazer, a pioneer,
In the face of adversity, she shows no fear.

From the Golden State to the nation's helm,
She stands resolute, overwhelming the realm.
A path paver, breaking barriers, setting the pace,
In the marathon of life, she runs her race.

In the annals of history, her name is etched,
Her story of triumph, widely sketched.
A path paver, a role model, a guiding star,
She shines brightly, no matter how far.

So here's to Kamala, the path paver, the guide,
In her wisdom and courage, we take pride.
A beacon of hope, a symbol of change,
In the book of greatness, her chapter is strange.

# Kamala:
## *A Beacon for Women in Leadership*

In time's annals, where stories intertwine, emerges Kamala,
Her journey divine, a mother, her love gala.
Not a sinner, nor saint, but a woman of might,
Her love for her nation, a beacon so bright.

Some may confound her, with women of past,
But her story is unique, a contrast so vast.
From the house of people, to Senate's grand hall,
Kamala's journey inspires, a lesson for all.

A sudden thought strikes, a plan takes shape,
With determination, grace, she makes her escape.
She brings her vision, her hope, her fight,
Pouring it out for nation, a beacon of light.

So plenteous her efforts, reaching far and wide,
Filling the nation with pride, turning the tide.
Some may murmur, some may commend,
But Kamala's resolve, it does not bend.

What makes her worthy of such high praise?
It's her unwavering spirit, her unyielding gaze.
Her memory preserved, transmitted with time's chronicle,
A testament to her journey, a narrative so supple.

Here's to Kamala, a trailblazer, a guide,
In her love for nation, we take pride.
Her story is not just hers, but a lesson,
A beacon for future women, answering the session.

In the end, it's not just about Kamala,
United by a mother's love, we stand tall.

Her journey, a roadmap for future women,
In pursuit of justice, our hearts enliven.

# Kamala:
## *The Trailblazer*

In the land of the free, under the western sky,
A woman emerged, aiming high.
Kamala, a name, a trailblazer, a star,
In the galaxy of life, she's come far.

Born of immigrants, in a land of dreams,
She navigated life's turbulent streams.
A trailblazer, breaking barriers, setting the pace,
In the marathon of life, she runs her race.

In the halls of justice, she made her stand,
Her voice echoing across the land.
A trailblazer, a pioneer, a guiding light,
In the face of adversity, she takes flight.

From the Golden State to the nation's helm,
She stands resolute, overwhelming the realm.
A trailblazer, a role model, a guiding star,
She shines brightly, no matter how far.

In the tapestry of time, her story is woven,
Her spirit unbroken, her resolve unshaken.
A trailblazer, a symbol of change,
In the book of greatness, her chapter is strange.

So here's to Kamala, the trailblazer, the guide,
In her wisdom and courage, we take pride.
A beacon of hope, a symbol of change,
In the book of greatness, her chapter is strange.

# Kamala:
## *The Dawn of A New Era*

In the land of dreams, under the golden sun,
A woman emerged, second to none.
Kamala, a name, a beacon, a hope,
In the canvas of life, she paints a broad scope.

Born of diversity, in a melting pot,
She embraced her heritage, forgot it not.
A beacon of hope, in a world so vast,
She stands firm, her roots steadfast.

In the pursuit of justice, she found her call,
In the courtrooms, she stood tall.
A beacon of hope, in times of despair,
She shows us how to love, how to care.

From the city by the bay to the capital's dome,
She carried her light, made it known.
A beacon of hope, in a world so bleak,
She gives voice to the weak.

In the annals of history, her light shines bright,
A symbol of change, taking flight.
A beacon of hope, in a world so vast,

In the theater of dreams, she's been cast.

So here's to Kamala, the beacon of hope,
With her at the helm, we know we can cope.
A symbol of change, a ray of light,
In the darkest hour, she's our sight.

# Kamala:
## The Change Maker

In the land of opportunity, under the azure sky,
A woman rose, aiming high.
Kamala, a name, a force, a voice,
In the symphony of life, she made her choice.

A child of immigrants, in a diverse land,
She took a stand, made her demand.
A change maker, she vowed to be,
In the pursuit of justice, equality, and liberty.

In the courtrooms, in the halls of power,
She bloomed brightly, like a sunflower.
A change maker, strong and clear,
In the face of injustice, she shows no fear.

From the streets of Oakland to the Senate floor,
She fought for justice, forever more.
A change maker, a song of hope,
With every challenge, she learned to cope.

In the tapestry of time, her voice rings true,
A melody of change, a vision anew.

A change maker, a beacon of light,
Guiding the nation through the darkest night.

So here's to Kamala, the change maker,
In her strength and courage, we find solace.
A champion of justice, a symbol of hope,
With her at the helm, we know we can cope.

# Kamala:
## *The Game Changer*

In the arena of politics, a change begins,
Kamala emerges, determined to win.
Not just a player, but a game changer,
Her vision for the nation, could not be grander.

Born of diversity, her roots run deep,
Promises to the nation, she intends to keep.
A game changer, breaking the mold,
Her story of resilience, needs to be told.

In the corridors of power, she makes her mark,
Guiding the nation, out of the dark.
A game changer, in a league of her own,
Her leadership qualities, clearly shown.

From the city by the bay to the capital's dome,
She carries her message, makes it known.
A game changer, in every sense,
Her dedication to service, her best defense.

In the annals of history, her name will shine,

A symbol of change, truly divine.
A game changer, making a difference,
In the pursuit of justice, she shows persistence.

So here's to Kamala, the game changer,
With her at the helm, we're in no danger.
A symbol of hope, a beacon of light,
In the game of politics, she's our knight.

THIS PAGE INTENTIONALLY LEFT BLANK

# Kamala

## *Dichotomy*

This chapter takes you on a journey through Vice President and Presidential Nominee Kamala Harris's unique identity, exploring her roles as a black woman, a daughter of America, and a beacon of hope. It delves into the dichotomy of her existence, reflecting the complexity and richness of her character. Through her story, we witness the resilience, unity, and hope she embodies. This exploration offers a deeper understanding of Vice President and Presidential Nominee Kamala Harris, highlighting her impact and significance.

# Kamala:
## *A Daughter Of American Soil*

Born on American soil, Kamala stands,
A woman of strength, meeting life's demands.
Her touch, a comfort, a source of might,
In America's journey, she's a guiding light.

Her kinship with us, a bond united,
Our spirits uplifted, our hopes ignited.
Drawing from the well of humanity's grace,
Kamala, a beacon, in America's space.

A daughter of America, also its mother,
Her role, her duty, unlike any other.
Her commitment, her resolve, so grand,
In her, we see America's helping hand.

Kamala lives, to our nation, she gives,
Through rises and falls, she persistently strives.
In our hearts, she ignites a light,
An American journey, she leads with might.

She is truly a woman, as she is an American,
And as truly an American, as she is a woman.
It is of her identity, we now speak,
Her touch strengthens us, when we are weak.

In the tapestry of America, Kamala weaves,
A story of hope, in what she believes.
Her journey, a testament to her might,
Kamala, a daughter of American light.

Kamala, a true daughter of America,
Her spirit, a melody, an euphoria.

In her, we see our nation's reflection,
A symbol of unity, of connection.

Kamala, a mother to all Americans,
Her love, a river, through our lands.
In her embrace, we find our strength,
In her journey, we go to any length.

# Kamala:
## *Her Blackness*

Kamala, black woman, strong, bright, her light finds,
In her blackness, she finds her light.
"Look upon me, for I am black,"
Her voice echoes, she lacks nothing indeed.

"Fair among women," others often do say,
Yet, she sees herself in a different way.
Her humility shines, a beacon so clear,
In her presence, fear we do not.

Kamala stands tall, yet bows her head,
In her humility, she is always led.
"Look upon me, for I am black,"
Her beauty, the world certainly does not lack.

Her skin, the night, her eyes, the stars,
Her strength has healed so many scars.
"Look upon me, for I am black,"
In her blackness, she certainly does not lack.

Kamala, black woman, a sight to behold,
Her story, a tale that must be told.
"Look upon me, for I am black,"
In her presence, we feel no lack.

Her blackness, a canvas, her spirit, the art,
Her humility, a melody, touching the heart.
"Look upon me, for I am black,"
Her beauty, nothing indeed does lack.

Kamala, black woman, a paradox, a mystery,
Her humility, her strength, part of her history.
"Look upon me, for I am black,"
Her presence, a sweet melody, does not lack.

"Look upon me, for I am black," she concludes,
Her beauty, our hearts, it never eludes.
Kamala, black woman, humble yet proud,
In her presence, we say aloud.

# Kamala:
## *The Love of All Americans*

Kamala's love unites all Americans together,
Men, women, young, old, light as a feather.
Rich, poor, learned, or still learning,

In their hearts, for Kamala, love is burning.
White, African, Asian, Spanish Americans unite,
In Kamala's love, they find the light.
From east to west, love so grand,

For Kamala, all Americans stand hand in hand.
Before divisions, unity was the scene,
In every corner of this land so green.
Chimes of unity ring out, love so pure,

In their hearts, Kamala's love is secure.
From every corner, people gather round,
Their love for Kamala, profound and sound.
America, in its glory, a sight to behold,

Their love for Kamala, a story to be told.
From every city, town, village, voices rise,
"Love Kamala," the heartfelt cries.
From every mountain top, a note so clear,

"Love Kamala," for all to hear.
No discord here, no jarring sound,
In love with Kamala, unity is found.
From sea to shining sea, people proclaim,

In every heart, Kamala's name remains.
The heart of every American, full of zeal,
In love with Kamala, a bond so real.
America says, "We are united, our spirit soars,"

And the world hears, "In love with Kamala, forevermore."
Her charm, like a radiant dawn, hard to ignore.
In every heart, her name, they adore,
A timeless love tale, adding to folklore.

# The Humaneness of
# Kamala

Kamala's passion, a beacon bright,
For nation's good, she fights the fight.
A thousand ways, her path unfolds,
In pursuit of a dream, she firmly holds.

Energy expended in a healthy way,
Uniting the nation, keeping disarray at bay.
A steam of hope, in hearts ignite,
For a future that's promising and bright.

Human minds at work, tongues in motion,
Employed for good, a potent potion.
A nation united, a grand objective,
Unused talents, a corrosive perspective.

Common humanity, Kamala's guide,
For the marginalized, she takes a stride.
Adapting herself, for others' good,
In their shoes, she has stood.

Like Apostle Paul, Kamala becomes all,
Helping others rise, preventing their fall.
A Jew to Jews, a friend to all,
Breaking barriers, making the wall small.

With children, Kamala becomes a child,
In their world, she has smiled.
With the aged, she shares their plight,
Guiding them towards the light.

Among the educated, Kamala chooses her words,
Among the illiterate, her voice is heard.

Prejudices faced, she does not jar,
Takes them as they are, near or far.

Seeking votes, Kamala shows the way,
To the election poll, come what may.
With a sorrowful spirit, she shares her pain,
Like a good Samaritan, in sunshine or rain.

A door to each heart, Kamala finds,
Entering with love, breaking binds.
Longing for welfare, a trait Godlike,
Snatching from inhumanity's strike, she takes a hike.

# The Kamala Dichotomy:
## *Human Being and Being Human*

In corridors  of power, a figure does rise,
Kamala, a name that in hearts, lies.
A human being, strong, wise, and kind,
In her, a unique spirit we find.

Yet, she embodies the essence of being human,
In empathy and grace, like a blooming camellia.
Not just a leader, but a beacon bright,
Guiding with wisdom, in day and night.

A child of immigrants, her journey began,
Under distant stars, to the American land.
Her heritage, a tapestry rich and diverse,
In every challenge, she did immerse.

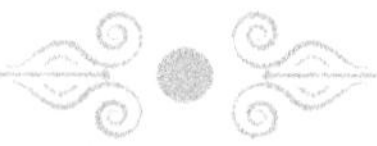

She stands tall, in the political sphere,
With courage in heart, and vision clear.
A human being, yes, she is,
But being human, is her true bliss.

In halls of justice, she made her mark,
Her voice, resonating, kindles a spark.
Being human, to her, means to serve,
To uphold justice, without any swerve.

Her name, Kamala, a lotus signifies,
Purity, beauty, in her, it lies.
A human being, in her role,
But being human, is her soul's goal.

So, here lies Kamala, in her might,
A human being, in the public's sight.
Yet, being human, is her true role,
A testament to her noble soul.

In the theater of life, two entities reside,
Kamala, a human being, with humanity as her guide.
To be a 'Human Being' is nature's right,
But 'Being Human', ah, it's Kamala's true delight.

# Kamala's Contagious Joy:
## *A Beacon in the Night*

Kamala's smile, a beacon in the darkest night,
Her laughter rings, a song so pure and light.
It spreads around, warming every heart in sight,
A contagious joy, dispelling gloom, setting all right.

In her presence, hearts lighten, spirits take flight,
Her laughter, a melody in the quiet night.
Echoing in the air, a sound so bright,
A symphony of joy, a beacon of light.

Her smile, a sunbeam breaking through the night,
Her laughter, a ripple spreading joy and light.
Dancing in the air, a sight so bright,
A contagious joy, a beacon in the night.

Facing despair, she stands upright, shining bright,
Her laughter, a balm making burdens light.
Resonating in hearts, a sound so bright,
A contagious joy, dispelling the long, dark night.

Her smile, a promise of dawn's early light,
Her laughter, a chorus of joy so bright.
Reverberating in souls, a sound that feels right,
A contagious joy, a beacon in the night.

Amidst sorrow, she shines so incredibly bright,
Her laughter, a symphony in the moonlight.
Echoing in silence, a sound so light,
A contagious joy, a beacon in the night.

Her smile, a ray piercing the dark night,
Her laughter, a melody of joy and light.
Dancing in the wind, a sound so bright,
A contagious joy, dispelling the long, dark night.

Facing adversity, she's a shining, guiding light,
Her laughter, a harmony in the starlight.
Resonating in the air, a sound so right,
A contagious joy, a beacon in the night.

Her smile, a sunrise after a long night,
Her laughter, a symphony of joy and light.
Echoing in hearts, a sound so bright,
A contagious joy, a beacon in the night.

In darkness, she's a guiding, shining light,
Her laughter, a melody in the twilight.
Dancing in the air, a sound so right,
A contagious joy, a beacon in the night.

# Kamala:
## *The Otherness that Unites*

Kamala stands alone, unique in realms of thought,
A beacon shining brightly, her own path she sought.
Her wisdom flows like rivers, free and unconfined,
In her, we see aspirations of our kind.

She treads paths untraveled, with courage in her heart,
Her otherness confuses foes, a strategic art.
Yet, she accommodates thoughts of others, wide and deep,
Sowing seeds of change, promises to keep.

Her otherness isn't hidden, it's a source of strength,
A wellspring of pride, it goes to any length.
In her difference, a common thread we find,
A beautiful tapestry of life, intricately intertwined.

To her soul's music, she dances, unafraid,
In her rhythm, her role in life is played.
Her otherness, a sweet melody in life's symphony,
In the grand orchestra, it's her unique harmony.

Kamala, the rose, blooms in adversity's soil,
Unshaken, undeterred, she stands, refusing to be foiled.
Her otherness, a testament to grace and dignity,
In humanity's garden, she has her own city.

Her otherness, she wears it like a crown,
In the face of doubt, she doesn't frown.
Like a phoenix, her spirit takes flight,
In the darkest hour, she becomes the light.

Her otherness, a prism of her existence,
Through it, the world gains a new persistence.
In her presence, we become aware,
Of the beauty in difference that we share.

Kamala, the dreamer, believer, and guide,
In her otherness, she draws us beside.
Her vision, a lighthouse in the dark night,
Guides us towards a future, bright and right.

Her otherness, a mirror reflecting our soul,
It reflects the truth, making us whole.
In her, we see the power of unity,
Under the same sun, in the same community.

In Kamala's otherness, we find celebration,
A testament to the diverse mind's creation.
Her journey, a testament to human will,
In her otherness, we find our thrill.

# Kamala:
## *A Journey of Discernment and Grace*

Mother of the nation, Kamala, wise and strong,
In discernment's depth, you truly belong.
Not just right, but almost right,
Your astuteness, a beacon in the night.

Curiosity, your guiding light,
In questions asked, you show your might.
In understanding, you find delight,
Your words, like stars, ignite the night.

Uncompromising character, your shield,
In moral battles, you never yield.
Trustworthy leader, truth revealed,
In your presence, doubts are healed.

Aligning mission with your core,
You lead with grace, and so much more.
In every act, your values roar,
Your influence, we can't ignore.

Courageous actions, calculated risks,
In your leadership, no asterisks.
Decisions made, no magic tricks,
Your discernment, a perfect mix.

Through failure, discernment grows,
In loss, your true strength shows.
With grit, you face all your foes,
Your resilience, to all, it shows.

Observing, synthesizing, you translate,
Information into action, you relate.

For those you lead, you elevate,
Your discernment, we celebrate.

Mother of the nation, Kamala, you're a star,
Your wisdom seen, both near and far.
In leadership, you raise the bar,
Your astuteness, is who you are.

THIS PAGE INTENTIONALLY LEFT BLANK

# eight

# Kamala

## Maternal Resilience

Welcome to the chapter titled "Kamala: Maternal Resilience". This chapter encapsulates Vice President and Presidential Nominee Kamala Harris's journey as a mother, a leader, and a beacon of hope amidst challenges. It explores her multifaceted roles as a mother in deed, a mother hen, a mother of multitudes, and a mother amidst challenges. It also underscores her dual role as a mother and a leader, her position as America's motherly beacon, and her stability akin to an oak in the political garden. Through her story, we witness the embodiment of maternal resilience, reflecting the strength of a woman who stands tall, guiding the nation through its darkest nights.

# Kamala:
## *The Dawn of Maternal Leadership*

In the land of the brave, the home of the free,
Arose a mother, strong as a tree.
Her name was Kamala, a beacon of light,
Guiding America through the darkest night.

She stood tall, with conviction in her voice,
A testament to the power of choice.
A woman in power, a sight to behold,
Her story, across the world, is told.

"Until I arose," she said with a smile,
"I carried my burdens, mile after mile.
But now I stand, a mother in this land,
Holding the future in my firm hand."

A world ruled by women, a dream so grand,
Peace and love, across every land.
For women abhor the horrors of war,
They yearn for peace, forever more.

In a world where mothers lead the way,
The dawn breaks on a brighter day.
No more war, no more strife,
Just the simple, beautiful, peaceful life.

So here's to Kamala, a mother, a guide,
In her wisdom, we take pride.
For in her rise, we see the truth,
The future is female, vibrant and couth.

# Kamala:
## *A Mother in Deed*

To Kamala, a mother not just in name,
But in deeds, in love, in enduring fame.
Not bound by blood, but by a bond much stronger,
Her care for the nation, could not be any longer.

A mother, she is, in every sense of the word,
Her voice, her actions, far and wide heard.
Not just those who birth, are mothers indeed,
But those who nurture, who plant the seed.

Nurses, governesses, teachers, and more,
Women of responsibility, it's them we adore.
God raises such women, time and again,
Their motherly virtues, not in vain.

They walk among us, these mothers so great,
Their love, their care, a perfect trait.
Even in youth, their motherhood shines,
In every action, in between the lines.

Motherhood, a journey, both long and wide,
In its cause, in its utility, they take in stride.
Such is Kamala, a mother so true,
In every action, in every view.

Here's to Kamala, a mother in deed,
Not by birth, but by every good seed.
In her care for the nation, she stands tall,
A mother to all, she answers the call.

# Kamala:
## *America's Mother Hen*

In America's heartland, Kamala, a mother hen, arose.
Once a prosecutor, now justice Kamala chose.
Kamala's readiness to serve shines like the sun.
From her people, Kamala hides none.

A beacon of love, Kamala symbolizes motherhood.
Her love for children, a universal good.
Kamala's love is dispersed, not divided.
To all her children, love is provided.

Like a hen, Kamala fosters, cherishes, protects.
Her love, warmth, care, she never neglects.
With her chicks, Kamala communicates pre-hatch.
A mother's love, no match.

In motherhood's quiet, Kamala keenly sees,
Which lullabies have the strongest pleas.
Kamala, the alarmist, tender and crunchy,
In danger, her protection is punchy.

Kamala sounds a caution, signaling danger.
She alerts everyone, even the stranger.
In America's corners, dreams are reared,
Her protection, a beacon, as it appeared.

Kamala, the mother hen, her wings spread wide,
Under her care, her chicks confide.
In her presence, they find solace,
In America's heartland, Kamala's embrace.

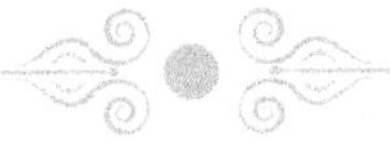

# Kamala:
## *The Mother of Multitudes*

In a world where many feel lost and weak,
A woman emerged, their strength to peak.
Kamala, a name, a mother, a beam,
Guiding the lost in life's powerful stream.

A mother not by birth, but by choice,
She became the comfort for those without a voice.
Nurturing, caring, always there,
Kamala, the mother who shows she cares.

She walks a path, both wide and steep,
Her resolve is strong, her heart is deep.
A path paved with love, care, and respect,
Kamala, the mother, we all reflect.

In the offices, in the halls of power,
She stands tall, every hour.
A beacon for the multitudes, a mother to all,
With Kamala, no one will fall.

From the Golden State to the nation's helm,
She stands resolute, her love overwhelms.
A mother's spirit, a nation's hope,
With Kamala, we know we can cope.

So here's to Kamala, a mother so grand,
In the hearts of the people, her love will stand.
The mother of multitudes, she takes her stand,
In the hearts of the people, her love expands.

# Kamala:
## *The Mother amidst Challenges*

In a world where challenges often hinder,
A woman emerged, kindling the tinder.
Kamala, a name, a mother, a light,
Against the odds, she takes her fight.

Not swayed by the powerful's might,
Nor by the skeptics' slight,
She stands firm, her resolve taking flight,
In the cause of justice, she ignites the light.

She walks a path, both wide and narrow,
Her faith in the people, straight as an arrow.
A path paved with love, care, and respect,
Kamala, the mother, we all connect.

In the offices, in the halls of power,
She stands tall, every hour.
A beacon for the multitudes, a mother to all,
With Kamala, no one will fall.

From the Golden State to the nation's helm,
She stands resolute, her love overwhelms.
A mother's spirit, a nation's hope,
With Kamala, we know we can cope.

So here's to Kamala, a mother so grand,
In the hearts of the people, her love will stand.
The mother for the multitudes, she takes her stand,
In the hearts of the people, her love expands.

# Kamala:
## *A Mother and a Leader*

In times of distress, when choices are few,
A mother's care is a healing dew.
Just as a child, in a mother's embrace,
Finds comfort and solace, a peaceful space.

In the realm of leaders, a pattern unfolds,
Of women at helm, as the story is told.
From Merkel to Ardern, to Tsai Ing-Wen,
Their leadership marked by the might of their pen.

Their nations thrived, amidst the storm,
Their early actions, far from the norm.
Lockdowns imposed, not a moment too late,
Saving lives, controlling fate.

In the face of risk, they stood so tall,
Their maternal instinct, saving all.
"Go hard, go early," Ardern's decree,
A mantra that set her people free.

In the absence of a mother, children may wane,
But with her return, they thrive again.
A testament to a mother's love,
A gift, it seems, from the heavens above.

So here's to Kamala, a mother, a guide,
In her wisdom, we take pride.
For in her rise, we see the truth,
The future is female, vibrant and couth.

In times of crisis, her readiness shines,
In every decision, her love intertwines.
A longing for a mother's care and embrace,
In Kamala, we find that grace.

# Kamala:
## *America's Motherly Beacon*

In the heartland of America, Kamala, a mother, arose,
Once a prosecutor, where justice she chose.
Her readiness to serve, shines like the sun so bright,
She hides nothing from her people, her truth is their light.

While she endeavors, with compassionate love as her guide,
To alleviate discord or trouble, she takes it all in stride.
She proclaims, "Until I, Kamala, arose as a Mother in America."
All thoughtful citizens echo this mantra, it's their panacea.

In the heartland of America, a yearning does grow,
For a mother's love, a comforting glow.
"Until mothers arise," the citizens plea,
Kamala, the true mother, hears their decree.

She believes in the worth of every soul,
No one is disguised, no one is a troll.
How valuable it must be, she does admit,
To prevent them from falling into the pit.

This work of prevention, a mother's privilege, it's lit,
To her is given the first opportunity, bit by bit.
Influencing the man or woman that is to be,
Laying the foundation stones of their future, you see.

To her is entrusted, this great America's fate,
Working out God's ideal, without any duplicate.
Upon her it depends, in this era's panorama,
Whether characters are noble or dwarfed by neglect.

It is a high privilege, a journey to start,
Guiding the immortal soul, playing her part.
And the mother to whom this privilege is accorded,
Brings to her work wisdom and knowledge, as recorded.

So here's to Kamala, the mother so true,
Guiding America, under the sky so blue.
Her readiness, her love, her grace,
In Kamala, we find, a mother's embrace.

# Kamala:
## *The Stable Oak in the Political Garden*

In the garden of politics, a mother stands tall,
Kamala, her name, echoing through the hall.
Stable as an oak, unwavering in her will,
Against the winds of instability, she stands still.

In the tempting garden of power, many sway,
Yet, Kamala's resolve, never led astray.
A mother to her children, stable and kind,
In her, a role model, they find.

Some, their ideas, unstable and inane,
Yet admired for persistence, despite the strain.
Kamala, her ideas, sensible and sane,
In the face of ridicule, her dignity remains.

The fickle, changing with the breeze,
Never admired, never at ease.
But Kamala, steadfast and true,
In her stability, a lesson to construe.

In the world's arena, instability is rife,
Yet, Kamala's steadfastness, a beacon in strife.
In the hearts of the people, her story dwells,
A testament to all, her story, forever tells.

Through the tumultuous times, her spirit prevails,
A stable mother in the political gales.
Her story, a beacon, shining bright,
Guiding us through the darkest night.

# Kamala

## Mother of the Nation

This chapter explores Vice President and Presidential Nominee Kamala Harris's journey as a mother, a nurturer, and a beacon of hope. It delves into her roles as a mother in deed, a mother hen, a mother of multitudes, and a mother amidst challenges. The chapter also highlights her as a mother and a leader, America's motherly beacon, and the stable oak in the political garden. Through her story, we witness the dawn of maternal leadership, reflecting the strength and resilience of a woman who stands tall like an oak, guiding the nation through its darkest nights.

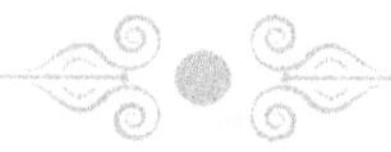

# Kamala:
## *Mother of the Nation*

In the heartland of the free, under the western sun,
A daughter was born, a journey begun.
Kamala, a name, a promise, a song,
In the land of dreams, she'd come along.

A mother's wisdom, a father's pride,
In her heart, they would always reside.
From immigrant roots, she drew her strength,
To reach for the stars, no matter the length.

In the courtrooms and halls of justice,
She fought for the voiceless, she made a fuss.
A mother to the nation, in deeds and words,
She soared high, free as the birds.

From San Francisco's fog to Washington's power,
Every step, every moment, an ivory tower.
A mother's love, a nation's hope,
With every challenge, she would cope.

In the corridors of power, a mother's heart,
Kamala, the nation's sweetheart.
Through trials and triumphs, come what may,
She stands resolute, day after day.

So here's to Kamala, the nation's pride,
In her strength, we confide.
A mother, a leader, a beacon bright,
Guiding the nation towards the light.

# Kamala:
## *A Mother's Womb Birthing America's Dream*

From Kamala's womb, America takes birth,
Her love unfurls, across the earth.
Wisdom guides our nation's flight,
In our hearts, her light shines bright.

Kamala's love, profound and deep,
In American hearts, its impressions keep.
Leaders come and go, their worth undeniable,
Yet, Kamala's touch remains, irreplaceable, reliable.

In our nation's deeds, Kamala imparts,
With a loving heart, tirelessly she starts.
The country turns, on her gentle sway,
In our affairs, Kamala lights the way.

Aid to her children, in despair,
Kamala, a friend, with love beyond compare.
When leaders falter, for reasons untold,
Kamala's tenderness, a sight to behold.

Translating lofty thoughts, into language clear,
Descending to our level, with a heart sincere.
Breaking wisdom's loaves, into crumbs so fine,
Feeding her children, on knowledge divine.

Nations stand, in their duty grand,
Caring for citizens, with a mother's hand.
Providing healthcare, economy, and more,
Striving for their children, from shore to shore.

Leaders serve, in their tender splendor,
As mothers, regardless of their gender.

America is fortunate, in this prime time,
To have Kamala, in her prime.

Kamala, compassionate and wise,
Teaches empathy's ABCs, under the skies.
Fierce, yet humble, in her heart pure,
Kamala, a mother to the nation, sure.

# Kamala:
## *The Nation's Nurturer*

In the vast amphitheater of our nation's heart,
Stands Kamala, a nurturer playing her part.
Not in the echoes of a cruel past,
But in the center of our present, vast.

She's not a sacrifice to popular fury,
But a beacon of hope, amidst the jury.
Not swayed by fleeting cause or applause,
But a steadfast believer in justice's laws.

She stands not to divide, but to unite,
In the pursuit of what is right.
She doesn't question where allegiances lie,
But asks, "How can our nation's hopes fly?"

In the fight against injustice and hate,
In the quest to make our nation great.
She nurtures the seeds of unity and love,
Guided by wisdom, like a dove.

She's not swayed by the crowd's cheer,
But listens to the voice that's near.
The voice of justice, truth, and right,
Guiding her actions, day and night.

She's Kamala, the nation's nurturer,
A leader, a guide, a sure harbinger.
Of a future where love overcomes strife,
And nurturing our nation becomes our life.

# Kamala:
## *A Mother's Love For Her Nation*

In world of love, hearts intertwine, divine,
Kamala, mother to nation, her love, divine.
Her love for people, love for the land,
A testament to service, steady as hand.

What are other loves, compared to mother's?
In Kamala's heart, no other love bothers.
She loves more than a leader, state figure,
Her motherly love for nation, no one can argue.

Character of a mother, deserving of affection,
Is mirrored in Kamala, in her direction.
Our whole heart is all too little,
In Kamala's love for people, we're guided, subtle.

Daily increasing in love, she gives all,
In service to nation, she stands tall.
Kamala believes, if not give all love,
You've given nothing, her love, a dove.

Though Kamala speaks with courage, fights for right,
Without love for people, it's a futile fight.
But Kamala's love is true, a living sacrifice,
Accepted on nation's altar, it's more than suffice.

Kamala, a mother, her love never waning,
In her heart, a love for people, reigning.
Her love, a beacon, in times of despair,
A testament to her spirit, beyond compare.

In the annals of history, her name will echo,
Kamala, a mother to nation, her love will grow.
Her resolve, her spirit, a beacon of light,
In Kamala, we find, a mother's might.

In the end, it's not just about Kamala,
United by mother's love, we stand tall.
Her love, a beacon of hope, light,
Kamala, a mother to nation, shining bright.

# Kamala:
## *A Mother's Love, a Nation's Strength*

Kamala, a mother, conceals nothing from Doug,
Gives no pledge of secrecy, sealing her mug.
In Doug's presence, listens to no praise,
Expresses to Doug every feeling, hope, phase.

Are there minor disputes, grievances in America?
Any American faults which annoy her, cause strife?
Does any American fail in duty? Differences emerge?
Threaten peace of America, under the skies' surge?

In disappointment, pain, smarting under injury's sense,
Kamala may be tempted to seek sympathy, hence.
By sharing her trials to some intimate friends,
Could be detrimental to her truest interests, sends.

Grievances complained of outside remain unhealed sores,
Kamala, wise woman, shares unhappiness secret with Lord.
While she strives, in every way love suggests,
To remove causes of discord, trouble, she invests.

So here's to Kamala, the Ready, the True,
A mother in America, breaking through.
Her readiness, her love, her grace,
In Kamala, we find, a mother's embrace.

Kamala, a beacon of hope, in troubled times,
Guides America with wisdom, as the bell chimes.
Her strength, her courage, a testament to all,
In her, America finds a pillar, standing tall.

So here's to Kamala, the Pillar of Strength,
Leading America, going to any length.
Her resolve, her spirit, shining bright,
In Kamala, we find, America's guiding light.

# Kamala:
## *The Mother of Unity*

In the heart of our nation, so vast,
Kamala stands, playing her part steadfast.
Not a solitary figure in a lion's den,
But a mother, a leader, among women and men.

She strides with purpose, her vision not confined,
A symbol of progress, with a resolute mind.
Not a victim, but a beacon of light,
Guiding us through the darkest night.

In the face of division, she calls for unity,
A mother's love, her immunity.
She stands not in fear, but in strength and grace,
A testament to the power of the human race.

She echoes the call of those who've gone before,
Her message of love, we cannot ignore.
In the landscape of our nation, she takes her stand,
A mother, a leader, guiding our land.

So here's to Kamala, the mother of unity,
In the heart of our nation's city.
Not a solitary figure in a lion's den,
But a beacon of hope, among women and men.

Kamala, a symbol of unity, in our nation,
Her love and leadership, a cause for celebration.
Her journey, a testament to her enduring spirit,
In the symphony of life, her melody we hear it.

# ten

# Kamala

## *The Echo of Yaa Asantewaa in Modern America - A Tapestry of Resilience and Love*

In this chapter, we journey through the annals of American history to explore the life of Vice President and Presidential Nominee Kamala Harris, a new heroine who embodies the spirit of Yaa Asantewaa, the legendary African queen. We delve into her journey, marked by courage, resilience, and an unwavering commitment to justice. We explore how Vice President and Presidential Nominee Kamala Harris, like Yaa Asantewaa, becomes a beacon of hope and a symbol of strength for her people. This chapter offers a deep dive into Vice President and Presidential Nominee Kamala Harris's life, her struggles, her victories, and the indomitable spirit that makes her a true heroine.

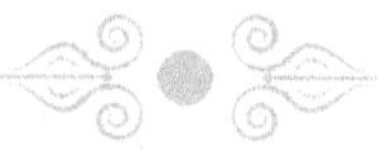

# Kamala:
## *The Yaa Asantewaa of America*

In the annals of history, a new tale is spun,
Of Kamala, our mother, the American sun.
Like Yaa Asantewaa, with courage in her core,
She stands for her people, she's the one we adore.

Yaa Asantewaa, the queen mother of Ejisu in Ghana,
Led her people with bravery, a fact we can't refuse.
And now in America, a similar spirit we see,
In Kamala, our leader, who fights for you and me.

She stands up to injustice, with determination in her eyes,
Like Yaa Asantewaa, she hears her people's cries.
She fights for equality, for a future bright and fair,
With the strength of Yaa Asantewaa, and a resolve that's rare.

In the heart of America, a new dawn begins,
With Kamala, our beacon, where unity wins.
Her children jubilate, their voices rise and fall,
In praise of Kamala, the mother of us all.

"Blessed, Blessed, Kamala," we sing with all our might,
Arise and lead us forward, be our guiding light.
In years to come, on solemn days, our voices will echo,
"May the spirit of Kamala continue to grow."

So here's to Kamala, the Yaa Asantewaa of our land,
Guiding us with a firm, yet gentle hand.
In the grand tapestry of time, her thread brightly gleams,
Weaving a future, that's the fabric of our dreams.

In the realm of justice, she's a shining star,
Guiding us towards a future, both near and far.

With every decision, with every law,
She's shaping a world, free of flaw.

Her voice, a melody in the halls of power,
In the face of adversity, she does not cower.
Like the steady current of a mighty river,
She's making changes that will forever deliver.

Kamala, a name written in the stars,
A testament to victory, over numerous wars.
Her story, a beacon for those to come,
A melody of triumph, a resounding drum.

So here's to Kamala, and her unwavering fight,
A symbol of resilience, burning bright.
In the canvas of history, her legacy shines,
An ode to her journey, in these humble lines

# Kamala:
## *The Chessboard Queen -*
## *A Dance of Power and Grace*

In the free land, a queen emerges,
Kamala, a name history purges.
Crowned Yaa Asantewaa of America, stands,
A beacon of hope in vast lands.

Her crown, not gold, but deeds,
Meeting her people's needs, she leads.
"I will," proclaims she with might,
"And they shall," under her light.

Yet, Queen Kamala knows her bounds,
Her royal words, not always resounds.
Understanding power's balance dance,
It changes at her term's end.

"Their wills," utters she with pause,
Knowing every action has a cause.
The wills of her children, free,
Are not hers to command, she agrees.

Yet, in strength, Kamala finds grace,
Leading with wisdom, not just pace.
Like a true queen, rules her board,
With love, respect, not just a sword.

In power's game, Kamala's a player,
With a mother's word, she's a slayer.
"I will," says she, not in boast,
For Queen Kamala, it's people who matter most.

"They shall," declares Kamala, with respect,
Understanding the human aspect.
Not like chessmen, moved at will,
But beings of spirit, hard to still. Amen.

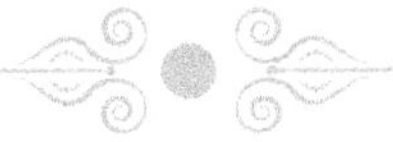

# Kamala's Strength:
## *A Mother's Fortitude in Divine Power*

Kamala, a mother, stands strong,
"Our sufficiency is of God," her lifelong song.
In the challenge to win a soul,
In God's sufficiency, she finds her role.

In the arena of politics, she fights,
Her love for her children, her lights.
With every battle, every win,
She echoes God's love, from within.

She draws her strength, from above,
In God's power, she moves.
Her fortitude inspires, her spirit soars,
In the face of challenges, she roars.

Her journey continues, her strength prevails,
In the arena of politics, she hails.
Kamala, a mother, her power unfolds,
In her strength, God's love she holds.

In the symphony of life, her strength resounds,
Guiding the nation, where unity truly abounds.
Her strength, a testament, that forever rings,
In Kamala, we find, a mother who sings.

Her love for her people, her dedication unwavering,
Kamala, a mother in politics, forever persevering.
In the grand tapestry of our shared history,
Kamala's strength shines, a beacon of mystery.

# Kamala:
## *The Tapestry of Resilience and Love*

From seeds of an immigrant's dream, a story,
Kamala, a beacon, her resilience journey told.
In corridors of power, voices often collide,
She stands firm, her convictions won't hide.

Born of an immigrant, her roots are strong,
Her faith in humanity, life's melodious song.
She looks to the world, finds hope in sight,
Guiding her children, with wisdom and light.

Her faith, a beacon, shining bright and clear,
In her heart, she holds children dear.
She whispers to them, "You're my joy, delight,
In you, I see a future that's bright."

Kamala, an immigrant, dared to dream,
Teaching her children, to reach extreme.
Her journey, a testament, to how far one goes,
From an immigrant's dream, to a leader who shows.

So, let's adore and bless, with gratitude,
Kamala, a reflection of an immigrant's fortitude.
In realm of service, where challenges are rife,
She shines the brightest, her journey, life's essence.

Kamala, a symbol of resilience, in our nation,
Her love and leadership, a cause for celebration.
Her story, a testament to her enduring spirit,
In life's symphony, her melody, we hear it.

Kamala, a mother, her love never waning,
In her heart, love for people, reigning.

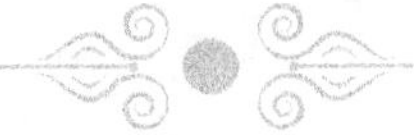

Her love, a beacon, in times of despair,
A testament to her spirit, beyond compare.

THIS PAGE INTENTIONALLY LEFT BLANK

# eleven

## Kamala

### *Our Momala*

In this chapter, we explore the journey of Vice President and Presidential Nominee Kamala Harris, affectionately known as Momala. We delve into her role as a mother, mentor, and guide, and how her love, ever true, shines brightly like a lighthouse in the heart of our nation. We examine how Vice President and Presidential Nominee Kamala Harris, as a sweet mother and a positive role model, shows divine love and lets this love shine in the hearts of her stepchildren. We also look at the impact she has on those around her through her mothering.

# Kamala:
## *Our Momala*

In heart of our nation, a beacon of light,
Stands Kamala, called Momala by stepchildren, shining bright.
A mother, a mentor, a guide, ever true,
Her love, like a lighthouse, always in view.

Kamala, our Momala, a mother so sweet,
Never tried to replace, but took backseat.
A positive role model, showing love divine,
In hearts of her stepchildren, she lets it shine.

She cooks as much as possible, meals a delight,
Her presence, her availability, a comforting sight.
She listens with patience, with love, with care,
In every moment of life, Kamala is there.

Her mothering matters, it's clear to see,
In lives of her stepchildren, in their glee.
So here's to Kamala, Momala so dear,
Your love and guidance, we hold near.

And one day, every American will look back,
Just as Lincoln did, in his own track,
"All that I am or ever hope to be,
I owe to my angel mother, my guiding sea."

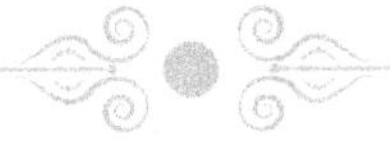

# Kamala:
## *The Blessed Momala*

In realm of stars, stripes, a radiant light,
Kamala stands, our Momala, a vision of might.
A mentor, a guide, a mother so true,
Her love, like a river, ever new.

Kamala, our beacon, praised by Kerstin Emhoff high,
Her virtues, wisdom, grace, reaching the sky.
Blessed she is, by those who know best,
Her virtues outweighing any given test.

Kamala's cheerfulness, a drumbeat, strong, loud,
Drawing all to Lord, away from crowd.
Her children, like olive plants, strong, able,
Rise in reverence, their respect stable.

They pray for her peace, prosperity, blessedness,
Pronouncing her blessed, in sincerity, no less.
For Kamala is blessed with spiritual blessings in Christ,
Her family too, having paid the price.

Doug Emhoff, her husband, praises her grace,
Her faith, love, humility, causing no trace.
So here's to Kamala, our dear Momala,
Your love and guidance, we hold, la la.

In tapestry of life, Kamala, our star,
Has left an imprint that will shine far.
Doug Emhoff, her husband, admiration in voice,
"Kamala, you are my heart's choice."

# Kamala:
## *A Momala's Warmth*

"Bask in Momala's love," motives for us all,
As her children, we stand tall.
"Bask in your mother's favor," friends call,
"Retain your position, from grace don't fall."

Momala, dedicated and true, not capricious,
Invites us to dwell in her countenance.
Always Momala's children, under her sky blue,
Live so as never to lose her dew.

Seeking warmth in winter, to Momala we run,
Advised to keep in her warmth, like sun.
Wisdom holds, if you lodge where love's none,
Might as well be in a chilly, fun-less land.

Thus is Momala's love, a radiant song,
"Bask in it," sun yourselves all day long.
Flowers teach us this, to the sun they belong,
Open themselves, turn their faces strong.

They love the sun, kissed by its beams,
Therefore, they keep themselves in its dreams.
When trees seek the sun, towards it they lean,
Do the same, in Momala's love be seen.

Our mother loves us; from love don't stray,
Forget it not, slight it not, let not fray.
Enjoy it, be warmed by it, light your way,
Be sanctified by it, every single day.

Momala, personified mother's love,
In her leadership, we take pride.

Guiding us forward, with a steady hand,
In her, we see this land's future grand.

Momala, America's mother, forever adored,
In her embrace, strength to explore.
With a mother's love, she leads our land,
Forever she stands, with a steady hand.

# Kamala:
## *Love's Pulse*

In corridors of power, voices often clash,
Kamala emerges, her resolve, steadfast and brash.
Not bound by duty's chains, nor head's beat,
But by pulse of love, strong, fleet.

Her journey, not calculated path, but heart's cry,
A testament to spirit, reaching for sky.
From heart's dictate, her actions take flight,
Guided by love, she champions what's right.

In world of numbers, where hearts shrink,
Momala's love for nation makes us think.
Not a matter of form, nor rehearsed part,
But spontaneous impulse of a loving heart.

Her story, a beacon, cutting through night,
Inspiring future women to join the fight.
In her love for nation, we take pride,
Momala, a mother in deed, our loving mother.

Facing adversity, Momala stands tall, strong,
Her love for people, greatest of all.
For the abused, marginalized, those left behind,
She fights for justice, with unwavering mind.

Her love, a pulse, beating strong, true,
Echoing in hearts of the red, blue.
A beacon of hope, a testament of love,
Momala, a love from above.

In every heart yearning for justice, every soul,
We see pulse of Momala's love, whole.
Her love, a rhythm, a constant beat,
In heart of our nation, it finds seat.

# Kamala:
## *The Heartland's Compassionate Mother*

In America's heartland,  Kamala, a mother, stands,
Her compassion for all, like eternal sands.
Unrestrained, her love, a river that flows,
Doug, her husband, in awe of her glow.

Radiant, Kamal, a momala, shines in trials,
Despite multiplied duties, her love compiles.
She may argue no strength left to give,
Yet in her actions, Doug sees love live.

Remarkable how presidency's burden seems to increase,
Yet Kamala, with love, takes it with ease.
Doug, her husband, amazed at the heavy load,
Finds in her strength, a comforting abode.

To noble woman carrying them, Doug sends love,
Heaven's blessing rests on you, my dear dove.
Of her who lives to do good, roams,
Kamala, true wife, mother, friend, sister, homes.

In power's corridors, her echoing footsteps are heard,
Kamala, a mother's heart, sings like a bird.
Her voice, a melody, in the nation's song,
A testament to a mother's love, deep and strong.

Through trials, triumphs, her soaring spirit prevails,
Kamala, a momala's hug, forever endures without fails.
In her, Doug sees our collective might's reflection,
A beacon of hope, shining with bright affection.

THIS PAGE INTENTIONALLY LEFT BLANK

# twelve

# Kamala

## *Virtues of Leadership*

This chapter delves into the life of Vice President and Presidential Nominee Kamala Harris, a leader who exemplifies optimism, love, faith, mercy, honesty, and respect. Her journey is a testament to these virtues, inspiring many. Her actions and words demonstrate how these virtues can overcome challenges and foster positive change, painting a vivid picture of effective leadership. Her story is a harmonious blend of these virtues, resonating with all who aspire to lead.

# Kamala:
## *The Symbol of Optimism*

In life's vast arena, multitudes subtly assemble,
Kamala emerges, a mother, her love doesn't tremble.
In modern world's hustle, a new story unfurls,
A leader named Kamala, in optimism, she whirls.

Her heart ablaze with love, pure and sure,
Facing challenges, with solutions, she does assure.
In this arena, many souls learn,
From Kamala's role, for whom hearts yearn.

We grow together until actions perform their earnest,
Doubts ready to burn, then faith fills the barn.
Examine yourselves, citizens, leaders, in faith again,
Leadership, more than a game, is not in vain.

In power's halls, divisions are but flowers,
When reckoning's day is near, action empowers.
Yet, among unconvinced, a division remains,
Opinions take many forms, like life's chains.

To those who reject her call,
This poem may your hearts enthrall.
In the end, it's about human essence,
Not political creed, but love's presence.

In life's symphony, Kamala stands tall,
Her love for nation, resonates above all.
Guiding with wisdom, serving with dedication,
Kamala, optimism's symbol, leads the nation.

# Kamala:
## *Beacon of Love and Humanity*

Mother's love, a flame, a beacon in night,
Kamala, mother to nation, her love, guiding light.
Just as sun's heat kindles fire in wood,
Her love for humanity kindles hope, understood.

What burns in her heart? Sun or wood?
It's love of God reflected, understood.
Her love, mirror of divine affection, bright,
Reflection of God's love, casting radiant light.

No one serves humanity, without love in heart,
Kamala's love for humanity, testament to her part.
Without love, where's zeal for glory, patience?
Without love, where's knowledge of right, essence?

Her love, test of condition, measure of grace,
When love burns, our nature blazes, space.
But when love smolders, grace is smoking flax,
Kamala's love never wavers, it's a fact.

Love must be maintained, life's primary necessity,
For Kamala, source of strength, cuts through adversity.
Here's to Kamala, a mother, a guide,
In her love, pursuit of humanity, pride.

Facing adversity, Kamala stands tall, strong,
Her love for humanity, greatest of all.
For the abused, marginalized, those left behind,
She fights for humanity, with unwavering mind.

Her journey, not just hers, but nation's tale,
A story of humanity, love, compassion prevail.

In the end, it's not just about Kamala,
United by love for humanity, we stand tall.

# Kamala:
## *A Faith Holder*

In a world where faith is often lost,
A woman held firm, no matter the cost.
Kamala, a name, a faith holder, a guide,
In the hearts of the people, she resides.

A nurturer not by birth, but by choice,
She became the voice for those without a voice.
Caring, loving, always there,
Kamala, the mother who shows she cares.

She walks a path, both wide and narrow,
Her resolve is strong, her heart is not shallow.
A path paved with faith, care, and respect,
Kamala, the mother, we all reflect.

In the courtrooms, in the halls of power,
She stands tall, every hour.
A voice for the voiceless, a mother to all,
With Kamala, no one will fall.

From the Golden State to the nation's helm,
She stands resolute, overwhelming the realm.
A mother's love, a nation's hope,
With Kamala, we know we can cope.

So here's to Kamala, a mother so grand,
In the annals of history, her name will stand.
The mother to the motherless, she takes her stand,
In the hearts of the people, her love is grand.

In the symphony of life, her faith resounds,
Guiding the nation, where unity truly abounds.
Her faith, a testament, that forever rings,
In Kamala, we find, a mother who sings.

Her love for her people, her dedication unwavering,
Kamala, a mother in politics, forever persevering.
In the grand tapestry of our shared history,
Kamala's faith shines, a beacon of mystery.

# Kamala:
## The Embodiment of a Mother's Mercy

In America, Kamala, a mother, arose,
Her gentleness, like the brightest gala, glows.
In every word, between the lines,
Kamala's love, like the sun, shines.

Kamala, a mother, wipes away tears,
In sorrow's times, her love appears.
In sickness, Kamala, a tender nurse,
Lifts the universe's heavy curse.

Upon her heart, burdens she bears,
Her love, a song, in words she shares.
When gloom descends, adversity strikes,

Kamala's faithful eyes, ignite like dykes.

Two stars of hope, in darkness shine,
Guiding the lost, to safety's line.
In dark hours, when burdens press,
Kamala's love shows its impressiveness.

An angel of mercy, Kamala, we see,
A beacon of hope, for you and me.
Kamala's mercy, knows no bounds,
Her love, like a river, surrounds.

Every home, a mercy house,
Where love's fruits, sturdy, grow and rouse.
Here's to Kamala, the Ready, the True,
A mother in America, breaking through.

# Kamala's Voyage:
## *The Power of Honesty*

In the land where courage holds its court,
Kamala stands, her tale of sort.
Her honesty, her radiant beam,
Steers her deeds, in daylight and dream.

She treads the trail that's fair and true,
Facing trials, her power breaks through.
Her might dwells not in sinew or stone,
But in her honesty, hers alone.

She upholds veracity, for equity she contends,
Her honesty her lighthouse, when darkness descends.

Unbending, unwavering, always resolute,
Her values she clings to, from root to fruit.

In the political arena, a daunting sphere,
Kamala's honesty stays clear.
She's an inspiration, for everyone,
Her character's strength, outshines the sun.

Her voyage sails on, her narrative unfurls,
Her honesty, more valued than pearls.
Kamala, a leader with power untold,
Fueled by honesty, brave and bold.

# Kamala's Symphony
## of Respect

In the grand orchestra of life's diverse band,
Kamala conducts with a respectful hand.
No matter the gender, race, or creed,
She values each note, each unique deed.

She sees not the status, high or low,
But the human spirit, in its glow.
Her respect is a melody, clear and bright,
Echoing in the concert hall of right.

From the highest mountain to the deepest sea,
She respects all beings, just as they be.
Her tune is one of dignity and grace,
A harmonious rhythm in the human race.

In the symphony of life, she plays her part,
With respect as the music, that guides her heart.
Her baton waves for one and all,
In Kamala's concert, none are small.

Her respect is her song, her powerful voice,
In the orchestra of life, her conscious choice.
Kamala, the conductor with a respectful tone,
In her symphony, no one stands alone.

# Kamala

## *Maternal Love in Politics*

This chapter explores Vice President and Presidential Nominee Kamala Harris's journey as a mother figure in the political arena. Her love, likened to precious pearls, serves as a comforting dome for many. Her unwavering dedication and service to the nation are testament to her guiding light. This narrative is not just about Vice President and Presidential Nominee Kamala Harris, but also about the melody of love that forever rings in the symphony of life, resonating with all who aspire to lead with love and service. Her story is a harmonious blend of these virtues, resonating with all who aspire to lead.

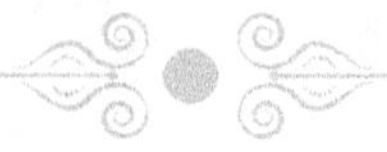

# Kamala's Love:
## *A Mother's Pearls*

In the world  of wisdom, with reverence we tread,
Our mother's love, like precious pearls, are spread.
Kamala, our Momala, her glow so divine,
Her love, like an alluring novel, forever shine.

Far from home, when we roam,
Her letters of love, our comforting dome.
Dictated with care, each expression, each line,
In our hearts, they eternally shine.

"And your mother expressly says," the preface so dear,
Treasured words, to our hearts they steer.
Repeated and cherished, again and again,
Her love, our refuge, in joy and in pain.

The love of a stranger, hollow and trite,
But our mother's love, the fairest of the light.
They are all diamonds, sparkling bright,
But Kamala's love is our guiding light.

Kamala, our Momala, your love we adore,
Like the Koh-i-noors of wisdom, precious evermore.
Your love, your guidance, your radiant glow,
In our hearts, forever they flow.

# Kamala's Love:
## *The American Spirit*

In times of danger, when fear is near,
An American, in mother's arms, sheds no tear.
Despite the threats, in chaos and commotion,
The American finds peace, free of any notion.

Just as chicks find warmth under their mother's wing,
We, the American people, to Kamala, we cling.
Our faith is steadfast, our resolve never weakens,
In God we trust, His protection never lessens.

There's a bond of love, a sense of home, a gentle touch,
A heart that cares, in all of us, it means so much.
Not just solace that brings a moment's peace,
But a mother's love that offers us release.

In the land of the free, America, our home,
Citizens stand united, no matter what may come.
Through storms and strife, in moments of dread,
Never have they wavered, never have they fled.

Americans, they're brave, not from power or might,
Not from the courage of heart, or the will's bright light.
But because they have a haven, a sanctuary so serene,
A God to guard them, and Kamala, the queen.

Kamala, the mother bird, with a heart so vast,
Leads her brood, America's cast.
In Kamala, they find solace, in Kamala, they find zeal,
For Kamala is their lighthouse, the one who seals the deal.

# Kamala:
## *The Dance Of Maternal Love In Politics*

In politics' dance, perspectives intertwine, lively,
Emerges Kamala, a mother, her love divine.
"Are we sole composers of policy?" she reflects,
Listening to diverse narratives, she connects.

She's not a soloist, but part of choir,
Her maternal instinct resonates, melody higher.
A leader, a mother, a lighthouse in storm,
In political symphony, she's a transforming form.

She recognizes understanding isn't hers alone,
It's shared stories of children, each unique tone.
In her maternal melody, leadership takes flight,
A beacon for all, as future turns bright.

Here stands Kamala, with empathy, grace,
Ready to serve, in relentless political space.
With a heart filled with love, spirit resilient,
She's more than a politician, she's brilliant.

Her journey continues, her maternal melody rings,
In lively dance of politics, where perspectives sing.
With each step she takes, with each policy,
She leads with love, steering nation with delicacy.

In grand orchestra of democracy, she stands,
Guiding the nation with firm, gentle hands.
Her love for her people, dedication unwavering,
Kamala, a mother in politics, persevering.

In life's dance, her love resounds,
Guiding the nation, where unity abounds.
Her love, a melody, that forever rings,
In Kamala, we find, a mother sings.

# Kamala's Love:
## A Mother's Song

In the nation's heart, Kamala stands,
A mother's love, extending hands.
Nurturing harmony, like a gardener's care,
Her empathy, a rhythm, in the nation's air.

Deeds are bridges built, paths paved,
Battles for justice, love's victories saved.
Kamala shares, with grace and humility,
Telling us, adequacy's not in utility.

Not in power, wealth, or fame,
Nor in the political game.
Adequacy is in silent prayers,
In love given, in burdens bearers.

In wiped tears, in shared smiles,
In kindled hopes, in dared miles.
Hearts, be not troubled, nor afraid,
For adequacy's in love, never to fade.

Serving with humility, leading with grace,
In every child's smile, in every embrace.
Thus, speaks Kamala, a mother's love,
Reminding us, adequacy is love from above.

In the symphony of life, Kamala's love resounds,
A melody of compassion, in which hope abounds.
Her song, a testament to a mother's might,
Kamala, a beacon, shining ever so bright.

# Kamala:
## *A Symphony of Love and Service*

In the realm of service, where challenges abound,
A mother named Kamala, in love, is found.
Her heart, a sanctuary, where compassion is the key,
A testament to love, as deep as the sea.

She gazes at her children, their faces shining bright,
In their eyes, she sees hope, a truly splendid sight.
Her love for them, not merely pity or mercy,
But a love that's as vast as the open sea.

Not just benevolence, not just complacency,
But a love that echoes through eternity.
A love intertwisted with her very being,
A love so profound, beyond all seeing.

In the quiet moments, when the day is done,
She holds them close, her precious ones.
Her heart whispers a lullaby, so tender and so mild,
Each note a testament of love for her child.

Kamala is their fortress, their guiding star,
Teaching them to dream, to reach far.
Her love, a melody, in their hearts will ring,

In the symphony of life, it's her love they'll sing.

So here's to Kamala, a mother so dear,
Whose love for her children is crystal clear.
In the realm of service, where challenges are rife,
She shines the brightest, with her symphony of life.

In the grand tapestry of our shared history,
Kamala's love shines, a beacon of mystery.
Her dedication, her service, a testament to all,
In Kamala, we find, a mother standing tall.

# Kamala's Melody:
## A Mother's Love in the Political Symphony

In politics' dance, where perspectives intertwine,
Emerges Kamala, a mother, her love divine.
"Are we sole composers of policy?" she reflects,
Listening to diverse narratives, she connects.

She doesn't claim to be a soloist, but choir,
Her maternal instinct resonates, lifting melody higher.
A leader, a mother, a lighthouse in storm,
In political symphony, she's a transforming form.

She recognizes understanding isn't hers alone,
It's shared stories of children, each unique tone.
In her maternal melody, leadership takes flight,
A beacon for all, as future turns bright.

Here stands Kamala, with empathy and grace,
Ready to serve, in relentless political space.

With a heart filled with love, spirit resilient,
She's more than a politician, she's brilliant.

Her journey continues, her maternal melody rings,
In lively dance of politics, where perspectives sing.
With each step she takes, with each policy,
She leads with love, steering nation with delicacy.

In grand tapestry of our shared history,
Kamala's love shines, a beacon of mystery.
Her dedication, her service, a testament to all,
In Kamala, we find, a mother standing tall.

In life's symphony, her love resounds,
Guiding the nation, where unity abounds.
Her love, a melody, that forever rings,
In Kamala, we find, a mother who sings.

# Kamala

## *Wisdom, Counsel, and Valor*

In this chapter, we delve into Vice President and Presidential Nominee Kamala Harris's wisdom, counsel, and valor. Her advice, drawn from personal experiences and historical lessons, serves as a beacon for many. Her words echo the values of truth, justice, and grace. This narrative is not just about Vice President and Presidential Nominee Kamala Harris, but also about the echoes of wisdom, counsel, and valor that reverberate in the symphony of life. Her story is a harmonious blend of these virtues, inspiring all who aspire to lead with love and service.

# Kamala:
## *A Mother's Counsel*

In the soft glow of evening, Kamala sits,
A thoughtful mother, her wisdom never quits.
Her children gather, stars around the moon,
She begins to counsel, her voice a soothing tune.

"Children, heed this counsel, let it guide your rise,
Deeds, like footprints, trace the path we devise.
Thoughts we sow, in minds, they rise,
As we give, so we receive, life's enterprise.

The world, our stage, decides the prize,
People reap actions, their scattering's size.
Admiration or scorn, world responds in ties,
Life, a journey, mirrors our enterprise.

Missteps, a detour, repeats, surprise,
Regret, its echo, follows its demise.
Life, a voyage, repeats, under skies,
Seed to tree, tree to seed, ties.

Yet, in journey, our joys arise,
World gifts happiness, in our size.
Loyal to humanity, it rewards our ties,
Cherish world, it cherishes under skies.

In universal guide, goodwill lies,
Misdeeds meet downfall, under skies.
In wrongdoing's face, justice applies,
A lesson for all, in humility rise.

Kamala speaks, "Children, learn from each sunrise,
Cherish each day, it's a precious prize.

In love and kindness, true wealth lies,
Live these truths, and you'll be wise."

# Kamala's Song:
## *A Mother's Wisdom*

In the heart of a nation, Kamala, a mother,
Guides her children with wisdom and charisma.
Her words, like a lighthouse, in political drama,
A beacon of hope in the panorama.

She speaks of Sarah, mother of nations, strong,
And of Hannah, whose faith grew long.
She invokes Ruth's strength, loyal and kind,
And Esther's courage, a rare find.

She speaks of Mary, a mother's love,
And Elizabeth, whose faith was above.
She tells of Rachel Carson, earth's knight,
And of Eleanor Roosevelt, showing her might.

She invokes names of women, old and new,
From Rosa Parks to Malala Yousafzai too.
Their stories of courage, triumphs, and trials,
A testament to resilience across the miles.

Kamala, the mother, shares these tales,
Her voice, like wind, fills the sails.
Guiding her children, the heart of the nation,
In hope they, too, will find their station.

In the political arena, where words have might,
She uses hers to shine a light.
A mother, a leader, a beacon so bright,
Guiding her children through day and night.

So listen to Kamala's song in the Lord,
Her words of wisdom to help you along.
For in each story, in each name,
Lies a lesson, a beacon, a flame.

# Kamala's Echo:
## *A Mother's Advice on Faith and Life*

In our nation's heart, a voice rings clear,
Kamala, a mother, on whom we depend, dear.
"Do not train young to set faith aside,"
"Embrace it, let spirit elevate," she guides.

Honor the Divine, acknowledge His teachings, guide,
Be teachable, accept His doctrine, coincide.
Many are trained to live by reason,
Setting faith aside, a spiritual treason.

Faith means this: Divine Word portrays,
Believe it; if meaning is beyond gaze,
Wait for further light, knowing it's true,
For it's the Divine who has spoken due.

Don't rush to judge, seek to understand,
In every situation, in every land.
Live by faith, not just by thought,

In everyday life, that's what we're taught.

Don't get lost in Divine's new ideas,
But by God's law, let life align.
Believe in truth, accept it, be light,
This is faith's path, the righteous fight.

Listen to this advice, guide your day,
In faith, wisdom, truth, don't stray.
Remember, you're never alone, even apart,
A mother's love is there, in heart.

In every challenge, in every chore,
Remember these words, let them be lore.
In pursuit of truth, wisdom, grace,
May you find strength, at your pace."

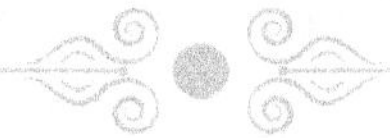

# Kamala's Wisdom:
## *Echoes of Valor*

In the heart of our nation, a voice rises,
A mother named Kamala, wise beyond years.
Her words, like a lighthouse, cut through guise,
A beacon of hope, dispelling our fears.

She speaks of Jochebed, Moses' mother, brave, true,
And of Lois and Eunice, whose faith grew.
She invokes strength of Zipporah, wise, kind,
And the courage of Rahab, a rare find.

She speaks of Michelle Obama, a profound leader,
And of Malala Yousafzai, courage did astound.

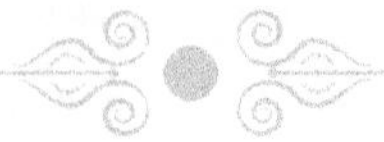

She tells of Ruth Bader Ginsburg, justice's feeder,
And of Angela Merkel, who proved her worth.

She invokes names of women, old and new,
From Sojourner Truth to Aung San Suu Kyi too.
Their stories of courage, triumphs and trials,
A testament to resilience, across the miles.

Kamala continues, her voice steady, clear,
Speaking of women, both far and near.
She tells of Marie Curie, unlocked radiation's mystery,
And of Amelia Earhart, soared through history.

Kamala, with wisdom, speaks of valor's echoes,
Of women who stood tall, against life's throes.
Their stories, she says, should inspire us all,
To rise, to strive, and never to fall.

# Kamala's Wisdom:
## A Mother's Advice to the Nation

In our nation's heart, a voice ascends,
Kamala, a mother, on whom nation depends.
"Cherish truth, justice, grace," she implores,
"Admit mistakes, for improvement soars.

Reflect on leaders confessing their wrongs,
Like Nixon, amidst Watergate, moved along.
Or Clinton, admitted his Lewinsky mistake,
Their humility in faults, a lesson, take.

Don't forget JFK, after Bay of Pigs,
Admitted the error, humility's lesson digs.

We uphold laws, confess their justice,
In humanity's goodness, we express.
Strive to better ourselves, for all to see,
A guilty heart honors truth, sets free.

Don't hesitate, children, admit your mistake,
No reparation for wrong, new path make.
The least and greatest thing you do,
Is to say, 'I erred, I renew.'

Mistakes are stepping stones in life's expanse,
Lessons learned, wisdom earned, in dance.
Take heart, stand tall, be brave, dear,
Perfection not the goal, strive without fear.

Our path towards growth, a better tomorrow,
In adversity's face, let's not wallow.
Rise, forge ahead, together we tread,
With love, kindness, empathy," Kamala said.

In history's annals, lessons we find,
From humble leaders, their errors signed.
Lincoln, a beacon, admitted Civil War's toll,
A testament to his strength, a lesson extol.

Gandhi, the Mahatma, confessed early failings,
Yet, his truth and non-violence path, sails.
Their humility, courage, a source of inspiration,
May their stories kindle in us, aspiration.

Mandela, resilience symbol, acknowledged radical past,
Yet, his freedom fight, forever will last.
Rosa Parks, a woman of courage, admitted fear,
Yet, she held fast, her message clear.

Their humility, courage, continue to inspire,
In adversity's face, they never tire.
May their stories kindle in you, fire,
To stand for right, may you never tire.

So, heed these words, children, let guide your way,
In truth, justice, grace pursuit, never sway.
Acknowledge mistakes, strive to improve, renew,
For this is growth path, this much is true.

In adversity's face, rise, do not fall,
With love, kindness, empathy, answer the call.
For you are future, our nation's hope,
To you, I entrust this solemn scope.

Remember, my children, you're never alone,
In our nation's heart, a mother's love is sown.
So, here's to you, to your journey, story,
May you carry these lessons, to your own glory."

# Kamala's

## *Maternal Influence in Politics*

This chapter delves into Vice President and Presidential Nominee Kamala Harris's maternal influence in politics. It begins with her loving response to her children's pleas. Her resolve to answer tough questions is highlighted. The dialogue she shares with her children is beautifully portrayed. Her enduring warmth, nurturing role in the political ecosystem, and healing touch in the political hospital are also emphasized.

## *A Plea From Her Children:*
# Kamala's Loving Response

In the nation's heart, Kamala stands,
A mother, heeding her children's commands.
"Craft every law to reflect God's love," they plead,
Kamala nods, "As you wish, it will be."

She's a beacon in the political landscape,
Her love for her children, her guiding cape.
Every policy, every law she crafts,
Echoes God's love, like comforting drafts.

Her children's voices, in her ears ring,
In the dance of politics, their words sing.
Every step, every move she makes,
Echoes God's love, for her children's sakes.

Her journey continues, her light never fades,
In the divine glow, her love cascades.
Kamala, a mother, her radiance beams,
In her beacon, God's love streams.

Her children call her, their voices rise,
In the dance of politics, she complies.
Every step, every move she makes,
Echoes God's love, in the wake of her strides.

Her journey is a dance, her rhythm flows,
In the divine melody, her love grows.
Kamala, a mother, her dance enchants,
In her rhythm, God's love grants.

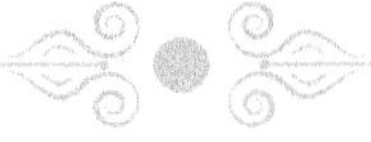

# Kamala's Resolve:
## *A Mother's Answer*

Kamala, having asked the questions, gives the answer,
In the political home, where challenges abound,
Stands Kamala, a mother, her vision profound,
Ready to lead, to serve, to enhance.

Yet nothing less will bring progress, it's true,
A chain of challenges, hurdles piled high, too.
No challenge can be dispensed with, no less,
Until Kamala arose, a mother, nation's progress.

All challenges of leadership, motherhood, overcome,
People's minds written upon by progress, some.
The stony heart has become a flesh tablet,
Leaders have been change's means, no less yet.

Since these feats have been achieved,
There must have been capability, believed.
In the means by which done,
Was it natural to leaders, or won?

Kamala goes on to answer,
In the quiet of her thought, under the moonlit span.
Telling us what that capability was not,
A journey of discovery, where it all began.

And these what things it was,
She unfolds, like a story from a forgotten lore.
In the heart of service, leadership, and inspiration,
She found what she was looking for.

She replies concisely to her own inquiry,
With a wisdom that's ageless and free.

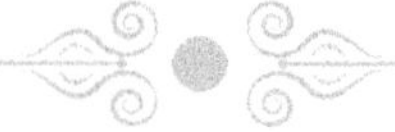

"It is the capability to serve, to lead, to inspire,
And to bring about change," says she.

# Kamala:
## *A Mother's Blissful Dialogue*

In the heart of a mother, a dialogue begins,
Kamala, a beacon, where love never dims.
Her journey, a testament to a mother's embrace,
Guided by the constitution, a human-made grace.

A mother's dialogue, a harmony so pure,
Resounds in Kamala's heart, forever to endure.
She cherishes the wisdom, the gentle interaction,
A mother's dialogue, her children's satisfaction.

"My children," she whispers in the soft moonlight,
Creating a haven of solace, holding them tight.
In times of joy, in times of strife,
She's ready for dialogue, it's her life's essence.

The glory of motherhood, she realizes,
In her moments of bliss, it's their love she prizes.
Her children, her own, a bond so precious,
In Kamala's heart, it's forever treasured.

"Behold, dialogue's bliss," she joyfully proclaims,
A testament to mother's love, life's games.
In understanding's realm, where wisdom flies,
She shines brightest, her dialogue's light.

Her children, her fortress, their guiding star,
Teaching them to dream, to reach far.
Their unity love, a melody, hearts ring,
In life's symphony, unity love they sing.

She sits with them, under moon or sun,
Engages in dialogue, until day is done.
A mother's dialogue, love's testament,
Guided by constitution, by those who went.

# Kamala:
## The Mother's Enduring Warmth

For Kamala, a mother so kind,
Her warmth for her children, we find.
Like a soothing summer's day,
It eases their wounds, keeps the cold at bay.

Mistakes made, under her watchful sight,
She guides them right, their beacon of light.
Through trials and tribulations, come what may,
Kamala's warmth remains, leading the way.

In every child's heart, her warmth stays,
A comforting presence, in countless ways.
A beacon of light, a guide so right,
Her warmth remains, day and night.

Manifestations of her warmth divide,
Into consolation and hope, side by side.
Everlasting comfort, a gift so grand,
Helps her children understand.

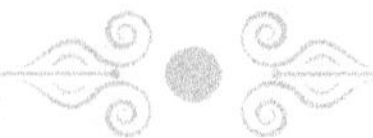

Her warmth, like a shield, guards from despair,
A constant refuge, showing her care.
Even when they stumble, lose their way,
Her warmth guides them back into the day.

In the face of sorrow, or joyous dance,
Her warmth remains, it's not by chance.
An enduring comfort, strong and true,
Kamala's warmth, a love that grew.

# Kamala's Garden:
## *A Mother's Nurturing in the Political Ecosystem*

Kamala, a mother, nurtures political ecosystem,
Her love for children, guiding wisdom.
"Can unity be cultivated alone?" she questions,
Listening to nation's rhythm, empathy blossoms.

She's not lone gardener, but diverse plantation,
Her maternal instinct resonates, blooming creation.
A leader, indeed, but first a mother,
In political garden, she's unlike any other.

Unity isn't solo cultivation, she perceives,
It's shared stories of children, each leaves.
In her maternal garden, leadership grows,
A beacon for all, her love overflows.

Kamala stands, with empathy, grace,
Ready to serve, she embraces space.
With heart filled with love, spirit bright,

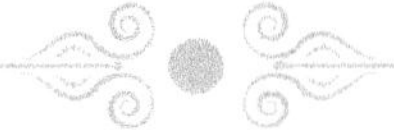

More than politician, mother, guiding light.

Her journey continues, maternal garden flourishes,
In political ecosystem, where unity nourishes.
With each seed sown, each bond's germination,
She leads with love, caring for nation.

Kamala, the gardener, tending to her land,
Nurturing each seedling, with a gentle hand.
Her garden, a testament to her care,
Blooming with love, hope, and prayer.

# Kamala's Heartbeat:
## *A Mother's Healing Touch in the Political Hospital*

In politics' hospital, where hearts are ailing,
Stands Kamala, not just a politician, unfailing.
"Are we sole healers of policy?" she questions,
Listening to nation's heartbeat, empathy connections.

She doesn't stand as lone doctor, but ensemble,
Her maternal instinct resonates, a balm so gentle.
A leader, yes, but a mother first,
In political hospital, tends to the worst.

She knows healing isn't hers alone,
It's shared stories of children, each tone.
In her maternal lullaby, leadership takes flight,
A beacon for all, shining ever bright.

So here stands Kamala, with empathy, grace,
Ready to serve, in relentless political space.

With a heart filled with love, spirit resilient,
She's more than a politician, she's brilliant.

Her journey continues, her maternal lullaby rings,
In political hospital, where healing she brings.
With each step taken, each policy's formation,
She leads with love, caring for nation.

Kamala, the healer, in her hospital stands,
Tending to each patient, with gentle hands.
Her care, a testament to her love,
Healing with hope, strength, and resolve.

# Kamala's Journey:
## *A Mother in the Fielding*

In the realm of politics, voices intertwine,
Stands Kamala, not just a politician, divine.
"Are we policy architects?" she ponders,
Acknowledging collective wisdom, her mind wanders.

She doesn't claim to stand alone, but amidst voices,
Her empathy resonates, in diverse choices.
A leader, a mother, a guiding star,
In political landscape, more than avatar.

She acknowledges understanding isn't hers alone,
It's shared experiences, in every tone.
In her empathy, true leadership emerges,
A beacon for all, as future surges.

So here stands Kamala, with empathy, respect,
Ready to serve, with an effect direct.
With a heart filled with kindness, spirit unyielding,
She's more than a politician, she's fielding.

Her journey unfolds, her empathy deep,
In politics realm, where voices seep.
With each step taken, each policy's creation,
She leads with empathy, steering the nation.

Kamala, the mother, in political field,
Her love for nation, like a shield.
With each word spoken, each action taken,
She shapes the nation, its core unshaken.

THIS PAGE INTENTIONALLY LEFT BLANK

# Kamala's Echo

## A Mother's Song, Compassion, and Humility

This chapter traces Vice President and Presidential Nominee Kamala Harris's journey as a mother in the divine symphony of politics. It begins with her song that echoes God's sufficiency and love. Her journey of compassion and understanding is beautifully portrayed. Her humility and confession as a leader are also emphasized. The chapter concludes with Vice President and Presidential Nominee Kamala Harris's testament to resilience in the face of pain and her role as a beacon of hope in the nation.

# The Song of Unity:
## A Tribute to Kamala

In America's heart, a mother's song begins anew,
Kamala, our beacon, where unity always wins through.
Children jubilate, their voices rise, then fall again,
Praising Kamala, the mother of all, not just men.

"Blessed, Blessed, Kamala," we sing with all our strength,
Arise, lead us forward, be our light's wavelength.
In future years, on solemn days, we'll remember,
"More of Kamala," will be our ember.

Notes of praise gather, like a flowing river,
As ages roll, their volume will deliver.
News rehearsals for the grand, we saw,
A unity symphony, that sweeps without flaw.

The novelty, jubilation, when the song is sung,
All of America, together, will have rung.
Understanding we share, truth we openly discuss,
"One blood made every nation of us."

No nationalities divide us, no interests part,
One blood, one people, one heart.
Here's to Kamala, our guide and mother,
In unity's song, in her we smother.

In nations' tapestry, in human kind's quilt,
Kamala, our mother, on your leadership we're built.
From sea to sea, from mountain to plain,
In every home, your legacy will remain.

Through trials, tribulations, victories, and strife,
Your unity song, Kamala, is our life.

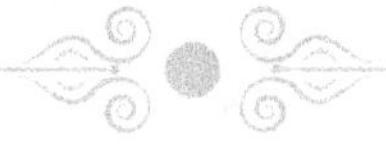

Here's to you, Kamala, our friend and mother,
In unity's song, your praises we smother.

Until Kamala arose, a mother in this land,
Uniting all her children, with a gentle hand.
Her unity song, a melody so sweet,
In our hearts, it echoes with each beat.

# Kamala's Echo:
## *A Mother's Song In The Divine Symphony*

In the symphony of life, Kamala sings,
"Our sufficiency is of God," her melody rings.
Despite the leakage, the cup is full,
In God's boundless grace, she finds the pull.

In the orchestra of politics, she plays her part,
Her love for her children, her art.
With every note, every chord,
She echoes God's word, in accord.

She harmonizes the nation, with her song,
In God's sufficiency, she's strong.
Her melody resonates, far and wide,
In the symphony of life, she's our guide.

Her song continues, her rhythm flows,
In the divine symphony, her love grows.
Kamala, a mother, her music heals,
In the echo of her song, God's love reveals.

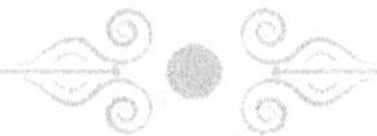

Kamala, the mother, her song's not done,
For the quest for justice is never won.
With each new dawn, she sings again,
A testament to resilience, in the face of pain.

Kamala's echo, a beacon of hope,
Helping the nation, with challenges to cope.
With God's love, her guiding light,
She serves the nation, with all her might.

# Kamala:
## *A Journey of Compassion and Understanding*

In life's grand tapestry, a story is woven,
Of Kamala, immigrant's child, resolve unbroken.
She stands not at power's throne,
But at each passing hour's crossroads alone.

Her journey began, as a new land child,
With Bible's teachings, she took her stand.
Guiding her children, with divine wisdom,
Kamala's path, a testament of time's prism.

The compassion of a mother, not first in time,
But redeeming compassion, as a sublime chime.
Her compassion, a starting point, a bright beacon,
Guiding her children, through night and season.

In quiet moments, when day is done,
She holds them close, her precious ones.
Her heart whispers a lullaby, tender, mild,
Each note a compassion testament for her child.

Kamala is their fortress, their guiding star,
Teaching them to dream, to reach far.
But also to understand enemies, forgive, forget,
A compassion lesson, they'll never regret.

Her compassion, a melody, in hearts will ring,
In life's symphony, it's her compassion they sing.
So, let us adore and bless, with gratitude,
Kamala, a mother's fortitude reflection, exude.

In service realm, where challenges are rife,
She shines brightest, with her life symphony.
Guiding her children to understand, even those opposing,
A testament to her strength, compassion forever growing.

Kamala, the mother, in her journey's echo,
Her love for nation, like a river's flow.
With each word spoken, each note played,
She shapes the nation, its future unswayed.

Kamala's journey, a testament to compassion, understanding,
In the political landscape, her influence expanding.
With each step taken, each challenge faced,
She leads with love, with God's grace.

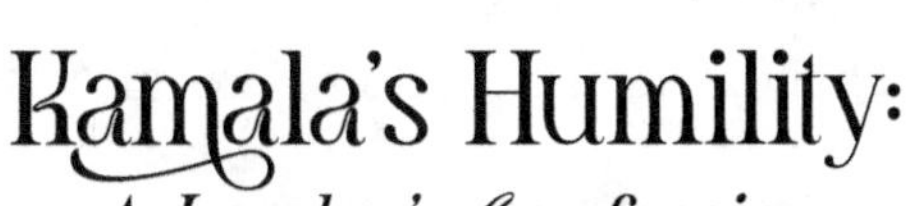

# Kamala's Humility:
## *A Leader's Confession*

"Not that we are versed in discourse," she professes,
In this moment, leaders disown political mastery.
Remember who it is speaking,
It is Kamala, a woman of tenacity.

She stands not alone, but with many,
Her humility shines, in a world lacking any.
A leader, a mother, a beacon bright,
In the political arena, a formidable sight.

Yet, she knows power is not her own,
It's the people's voice, in every tone.
In her humility, her true strength unfurls,
A lesson for us, in this complex world.

So here stands Kamala, with humility, grace,
Ready to lead, in this relentless race.
With a heart full of passion, spirit free,
She's more than versed, for you and me.

Kamala, the mother, her journey's not done,
For the quest for justice is never won.
With each new dawn, she rises again,
A testament to resilience, in the face of pain.

Kamala's humility, a beacon of hope,
Helping the nation, with challenges to cope.
With God's love, her guiding light,
She serves the nation, with all her might.

Kamala, the mother, in her journey's echo,
Her love for nation, like a river's flow.
With each word spoken, each note played,
She shapes the nation, its future unswayed.

# Voices of Valor

## Kamala's Tribute to Heroines and Founding Fathers

This chapter presents Vice President and Presidential Nominee Kamala Harris's homage to heroines and founding fathers, her heartfelt melody, and motherly wisdom. She honors the courage and resilience of historical women, acknowledges the vision of the founding fathers, and shares her love for the nation. Vice President and Presidential Nominee Kamala Harris also imparts wisdom, emphasizing truth, justice, and the courage to admit mistakes. This chapter is a testament to the power of learning from the past and aspiring for a better future.

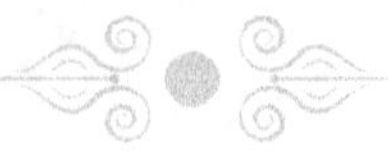

# Kamala:
## *A Reflection of Historic Love*

In the tapestry of time, a tale unfolds,
Of Kamala, a mother, whose love never old.
She stands with the divine, in concert, holy,
Her actions, a testament of love, never overtly.

She is a gift, a beacon of love,
Guiding her children, with wisdom from above.
Just as Martha Washington, Abigail, and Elizabeth,
Loved their children, Kamala too, would pay any depth.

In Kamala's heart, a love story is written,
A tale of love, by no hardship smitten.
Like Eleanor Roosevelt, Jackie Kennedy, Michelle Obama,
Her love is a soothing, healing, calming balm.

The love of the divine, not from one,
Echoes in Kamala's heart, answering a sacred call.
Sojourner Truth, Harriet Tubman, Susan B. Anthony,
Their love is undivided, in Kamala's love, it's confided.

In the annals of history, her love will shine,
A beacon of hope, forever divine, so fine.
Just as Rosa Parks, Maya Angelou, Oprah Winfrey,
Kamala's love is a testament to their legacy.

One love dwells in the heart of women,
A love mirrored in Kamala, for all to see.
So, let us adore and bless, with gratitude,
Kamala, a reflection of historic love, in multitude.

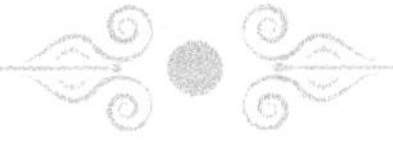

# Kamala's Tapestry:
## *A Tribute to Women of Valor*

In time's grand tapestry, woven thread by thread,
Stand women of stature, path we tread.
Susan B. Anthony, with her voice strong,
Mae Jemison in space, where no woman belonged.

Ellen Johnson-Sirleaf took helm in Liberia,
Her leadership a beacon in the realm.
Christine Lagarde stood with integrity,
Served Liberia for the greater good, effectively.

Phumzile Mlambo-Ngcuka shone in diplomacy,
Represented Ethiopia on the global stage, exclusively.
Sahle-Work Zewde found her call in education,
Served Ethiopia, helping all without hesitation.

Samia Suluhu Hassan grew in politics,
As Tanzania's first female VP, she ticks.
Mariam Chabi Talata led in Parakou,
As city councillor, fed her people too.

Mutale Nalumango thrived in government,
Under Mwanawasa's rule, her career was spent.
Rebecca Nyandeng De Mabior rose in South Sudan,
As fourth VP, she faced every ban.

Ellen Johnson Sirleaf ran in Liberia, undeterred,
Despite civil war, her plan occurred.
Joyce Hilda Banda cared for rural poor,
Shared her vision with Business Women's Association tour.

Catherine Samba-Panza served in Bangui,
Appointed as mayor, she never took a dig.

Then came Kamala, a mother wise,
United her children under American skies.

In her, reflections of those before,
Women of courage who opened the door.
Here's to the women who made history,
Their stories, a testament to their victory.

To Kamala, who now stands tall,
We honor you, to your strength we fall.
In your journey, many barriers you broke,
Your success, a beacon of hope, it spoke.

# Kamala's Song:
## *A Beacon Amidst the Storm*

In the heart of our nation, Kamala stands tall,
A beacon of hope, for one and all.
When her children fall, in fear or despair,
She lifts them up, with wisdom and care.

Just as Susan B. Anthony fought for women's right,
And Clara Barton, nursed the wounded in the night,
Kamala does the same, her love so strong,
Guiding us through life, helping us belong.

She speaks of faith, of a promise divine,
That God will save the humble, in time.
When the world is engulfed in fear and dread,
She assures us of a lifting up, instead.

Just as Marie Curie, in the lab, found radium's grace,

And Rosa Parks, in the bus, claimed her rightful place,
Kamala guides us through the stormy night,
With her words of comfort, her guiding light.

She reminds us of the difference, clear and bright,
Between those who walk in darkness, and those in light.
When tribulations come, as they surely might,
She assures us of a lifting up, a beacon in the night.

Just as Helen Keller, with her words, found favor,
And Margaret Thatcher, amidst the oppressed, a love to savor,
So too, Kamala assures us, amidst our woes,
That there will be a lifting up, as the river of providence flows.

If the earth should rock and reel, if the sun should dim,
If the moon turns to blood, if the stars grow dim,
Fear not, for you will be caught up to Him,
Or safe under heaven, singing the victory hymn.

In every challenge, in every chore,
Remember these words, let them be your lore.
In the pursuit of truth, wisdom, and grace,
May you find strength, at your own pace.

So here's to Kamala, a mother true,
Not by birth, but by actions, through and through.
In the heart of our nation, her voice rings clear,
"There is lifting up," she says, "Have no fear."

Like Eleanor Roosevelt, a woman so brave,
Who stood up for human rights, a path for girls she paved.
Kamala, too, lifts us up, when we fall,
A mother to all, she answers the call.

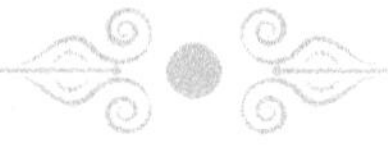

# Kamala's Homage
## *to Heroines*

Kamala, a heroine, for generations to come,
Her wisdom, her strength, second to none.
She speaks of heroines, their stories unfurled,
Their courage, their fight, changing the world.

She speaks of Harriet Tubman, led slaves to freedom,
And of Mother Teresa, who served the poor.
Invokes Rosa Parks' courage, who took a stand,
And Jane Goodall, who protected the land.

Tells of Florence Nightingale, nursed the sick, wounded,
And Malala Yousafzai, whose courage is astounded.
Speaks of Wangari Maathai, planted trees for earth,
And Benazir Bhutto, who proved her worth.

Invokes names of women, both old and new,
From Frida Kahlo to Maya Angelou.
Speaks of Mary Magdalene, a follower true,
And Mary, nurtured the Savior of the world.

Then speaks of Hillary Clinton, power and grace,
Stood in political arena, ran the race.
Their stories, a testament to resilience, might,
A beacon for all, shining bright.

Listen, dear children, to Kamala's wise refrain,
Her wisdom, a compass, in sunshine and rain.
In these women's lives, in each story,
Lies a path to honor, to glory.

Kamala's voice rises, echoing through the hall,
"Learn from these heroines, stand tall.

Their courage, their strength, let it inspire,
To reach for your dreams, aspire higher."

# Kamala's Homage:
## *A Tribute to the Founding Fathers*

I, Kamala, a humble daughter of the nation,
Speak to you, my children, with deep admiration.
In the spirit of our founding fathers, let us unite,
In acknowledging God's rule, let us ignite.

Our founding fathers, brave and true,
Built this nation, for me and you.
They were God's creatures, this truth they embraced,
In their hearts, His love, they traced.

They acknowledged His rule, though it was hard,
In every law, in every yard.
They honoured God, in thought, word, and deed,
For in honoring Him, they found all they need.

They dared and died in their loyalty to the Lord,
Their supreme Lord, their accord.
They did not breathe apart from Him,
Their lights never dim.

They honoured God with obedience, joyous and definite,
Prompt and constant, as grace helped them commit.
So, my children, as you journey through,
Remember these truths, they'll guide you through.

Our founding fathers, in unity they stood,

For freedom and justice, for the greater good.
Their vision and foresight, their sacrifice and pain,
Laid the foundation, for our nation's gain.

They dreamt of a land, free and fair,
A place of hope, beyond compare.
Their legacy lives on, in every law, every right,
In the spirit of liberty, in the pursuit of light.

So, my children, as you walk this land,
Remember the sacrifices, of the founding band.
Their courage, their wisdom, their unwavering might,
Let it guide you, let it be your light.

#  Kamala:
## *The Heart's Uncharted Melody*

In the realm of power, where voices often clash,
Kamala emerges, her love making a splash.
Not bound by duty's chains, nor by the mind's decree,
But by the heart's own song, wild and free.

Her journey, not a mimicry of those before,
But a heart's fervent cry, a lore.
From the heart's whisper, her actions take flight,
Guided by love, she champions the right.

In a world of echoes, where hearts often shrink,
Kamala's love for her nation paints a vibrant ink.
Not a matter of form, nor a rehearsed part,
But the spontaneous rhythm of a loving heart.

Her tale, a symphony, resonating in the silent night,
Inspiring future women to join the fight.
In her love for her nation, we find our stride,
Kamala, a guiding star, our trusted guide.

In the face of adversity, Kamala stands tall,
Her love for her people, the greatest of all.
She fights for justice, with an unwavering mind,
A beacon of hope, a testament of love, we find.

Her love, a pulse, beating strong and true,
Echoing in the hearts of the red, white, and blue.
A beacon of hope, a testament of love,
Kamala, a guiding star above.

Her love, a rhythm, a constant beat,
In the heart of our nation, it finds its seat.
Her journey, a melody that continues to play,
Inspiring future women, leading the way.

THIS PAGE INTENTIONALLY LEFT BLANK

# Kamala 's Plea

## A Mother's Prayer For Unity And Truth

This chapter delves into the heartfelt prayers of Vice President and Presidential Nominee Kamala Harris, reflecting her deep concern for her children and the nation. It explores her pleas for truth, unity, sincerity, gentleness, and divine obedience. The chapter underscores her faith in divine providence and her commitment to embodying these virtues in her service to the nation. It concludes by celebrating Vice President and Presidential Nominee Kamala Harris's impact as a symbol of strength, unity, and motherly love.

# Kamala's Plea
## *A Prayer for Truth and Unity in our Current World*

In the quiet of the night, Kamala kneels,
Her voice echoes softly, a whisper that heals.
In the stillness around her, her faith stands bright,
A beacon of hope in the dark of the night.

"O Loving Father, hear my plea,
For my children, our nation, for all to be free.
From the shackles of our times, may we rise,
Guided by truth, under Your wise skies.

Preserve us, O Lord, from unity blind,
Where truth is lost, and principles maligned.
May noble virtues not be masked by pretense,
Nor charity become an effeminate defense.

Deliver us, O Lord, from indifference to Your will,
That freezes our hearts, like an iceberg still.
Save us from actions that harm peace, so rife,
That threatens to engulf us, in strife.

Protect us from evils, like hatred and disunity,
That plague our world with such impunity.
From behaviors that disrupt harmony and foster fear,
And from the sin pandemic's unending disaster, so near.

May You send priests, who'll rise above,
Echoing Your word, with a voice of love.
'Let us turn back, for our path has been misled,
And our pact with darkness, shall no longer be fed.'

May there be women, strong as Deborah, wise as Miriam,
Who denounce all league with error, under the sky's diadem.
Who declare that compromise with sin, is God's abhorrence,
And stand firm in truth, with divine perseverance."

# Kamala's Prayer
## *A Mother's Plea for Unity Among all Races*

In that quiet moment, Kamala, the mother, continue her prayer,
"Father God I humbly raise my voice to You,
Hear my plea, let Your love shine.
For every race under the sun,
In Your eyes, we are all one.

For myself, my children, my nation, and all humanity,
I pray for unity, love, peace.
Though of Indian descent, I stand for all,
Jews, Africans, Asians, Caucasians, big and small.

White, Black, Poor, Rich, Young, Old,
Every human story, yet to be told.
For myself, my children, my nation, and all humanity,
I pray for unity of God's creed, and for unity in diversity.

In every corner of our world, near and far,
Each race stands distinct, like a singular star.
Yet connected we are, by bonds unseen,
In the grand cosmic dance, in the divine routine.

Not a cluster of races as one entity,
But a constellation of races, in divine plurality.

Disunity is not what God's Spirit seeks,
In the grandeur of humanity, diversity peaks.

People of different hues, cultures unique,
Each race contributes to the mystique.
In the human race, no uniformity I find,
Each race is distinct, yet of the same kind.

One race, diverse opinions, yet one world,
Each race has its own rhythm, its own design.
Unity of the Spirit, in love it's manifested,
Across miles and oceans, it's never bested.

From every race and every creed,
In love as brethren, in Spirit we're free.
Their spiritual welfare, to me, is dear,
In the unity of the Spirit, we're all near.

So, I pray for unity, for love, for peace,
For a world where divisions cease.
May understanding replace all strife,
Bringing harmony to every life."

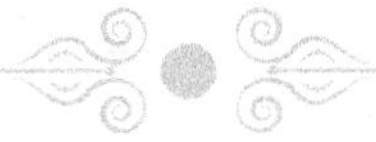

# Kamala's Supplication
## *A Mother's Prayer*

In the hush of dawn, Kamala kneels,
A mother's heart, her prayer reveals.
"Oh Father, Your grace to mankind, it heals,
No eloquence needed, Your love, it feels.

You etch a path for the gentle rain's start,
Nourishing the fields, Your heavenly art.
Who but You could play this part?
Without You, how could life impart?

Thrice-holy Father, with sinners, You deal,
Provoked to wrath, yet mercy, You reveal.
How could the Judge, in justice real,
Overlook our sins, yet love still feel?

A question posed, seraphim confound,
In celestial conclave, no answer found.
"How can Father justify, yet justice abound?"
A mystery deep, in wisdom profound.

Infinite wisdom found the way,
Through the Son's sacrifice, salvation lay.
"Chastisement of our peace," they say,
"By His stripes, we're healed today."

I, Kamala, pray for myself and nation,
For my children, in humble supplication.
Father's grace, a heavenly proclamation,
Guides us all, in His creation."

# Kamala's Plea
## A Mother's Appeal for Grace for her Children and Country

Kamala, a mother, at dawn's break, prays,
For her children and country, her plea conveys.
"Oh Father, it is You who grace bestows,
To all of humanity, Your mercy flows.

Blessed be You, Father, for this divine design,
May Your name be revered, by every human line.
You've chosen to give grace to man,
Crafted a conduit for Your grace to span.

Never overlooked, Your grace's course,
Guiding all grace that comes with force.
Like a waterway for each raindrop's sway,
From sky to earth, they find their way.

Not a speck of rain falls off track,
Each drop navigated by You, there's no lack.
Like celestial bodies in their orbits, they comply,
Your purpose guides each snowflake from the sky.

All orchestrated by Your timeless decree,
Only God can arrange this with such proficiency.
The world is hydrated, not to overwhelm,
But gently, drop by drop, Your purpose at the helm.

Raindrops cling to blades of grass,
Neither too hefty nor too scant, just the right class.
Like radiant gems on hedgerows amass,
So is Your grace, given sovereignly and wise, no impasse.

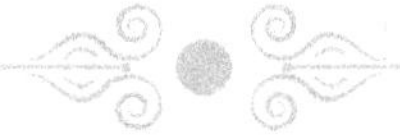

I, Kamala, appeal for my children and country,
In humble plea, I make this entreaty.
May Father's grace, a heavenly declaration,
Guide us all, in this great country."

# Kamala's Prayer
## *A Mother's Prayer for Protection*

As dawn breaks, Kamala, continues to pray,
For my children and our nation, in every way.
"Oh Father, it is You who calms the sea,
In times of danger, Your grace is our decree.

When tempests rage and billows roar,
We trust in You, our hearts implore.
He who holds the waters in His hand,
Will protect us, on sea or land.

In the midst of life's storms, we find our station,
Waiting for Father's will, calm and serene,
Whether to reach heaven's port, or life's scene.

We know the storm is held by You,
Nothing can harm us, nothing untrue.
On dry land too, Your comfort we find,
In times of storm, You calm the mind.

When thunder shakes the earth, and lightning flashes,
We walk in the open, amidst the crashes.
Looking up to the heavens, gates opening wide,
In Your presence, we confide.

We hear our heavenly Father's voice,
In Your nearness, we rejoice.
You would not hurt the children of Your love,
Your nature kind, Your covenant above.

Not just from commotions in the physical sphere,
But in all life's trials, You are near.
May Your protection be our shield,
In Your grace, our fears are healed."

# Kamala's Supplication
## *A Prayer for Godliness*

In the quiet of dawn, Kamala prays,
For her children, her nation, always.
"Oh Father, Saviour, Propitiation for sin,
Help us trust You, let godliness begin.

Not all are godly, alas, it's true,
The ungodly many, the godly few.
But those who fear You, desire to know,
Have a measure of godliness, a blessed glow.

May we be like those, communion constant,
Whose prayers and tears to You are instant.
Who sigh for deeper acquaintance with You,
May we be godly, in higher view.

Oh Father, by continual fellowship we seek,
Help us become like You, humble, meek.
Upon whom the image of Christ is cast,

May we  look on Him long, hold  Him fast.

May we find You everywhere, all we see,
In all Your works, in every tree.
May we trace everything to You, joy and pain,
Look to You for everything, loss and gain.

May we be those who live for You alone,
To whom You are joy, our cornerstone.
The help and the health of our countenance bright,
May we dwell in You, in Your holy light.

Father, may this nation be filled with godly,
Men and women, who dwell in godly character.
In Your good time, may we be called away,
To see You, rejoice before You, in eternal day."

# Kamala's Plea
## A Mother's Plea for Sincerity

I, Kamala, a mother, as dawn unfolds, intercede,
For my children and our nation, sincerity we need.
"Oh Father, the Just One, the Truth, the Light,
Help us be sincere, in Your holy sight.

Our nation, in its present state, I consider,
We appeal to You, in matters solemn and tender.
The insincere mimic the Christian's grace,
But lack the fruits of the Spirit, leave a trace.

In all deceptions, a weak point is the mission,
A sincere heart, in prayer, is the vision.

May we be those who pray with sincerity,
In Jesus Christ a new creature, in Your vicinity.

Father, may this nation be filled with sincerity,
Men and women, children, in their entirety.
In Your grace, may we be led,
To see You, rejoice before You, in eternal stead.

May we walk in truth, shun the insincere,
In our words and actions, let honesty appear.
Father, guide us in Your ways,
In sincerity and truth, all our days.

May we walk in truth, shun the insincere,
In our words and actions, let honesty appear.
Father, guide us in Your ways,
In sincerity and truth, all our days.

I pray for my children, in their current state,
May they walk in sincerity, may they never deviate.
And for our nation, in its complexity,
May sincerity prevail, in its entirety."

In the hush of dawn, Kamala, a mother, prays,
For her children, for our nation, for gentleness always.
"Oh Father, the Source of Love, the Beacon of Hope,
Guide us to embody gentleness, give us the scope.

In this diverse nation, where discord often reigns,
Help us be gentle, when conflict strains.
The hard-hearted may mimic the Christian's grace,
But lack the fruits of the Spirit, leave a trace.

In our relationships, a gentle heart is the mission,
In prayer, it's the vision, in action, it's the decision.

May we be those who pray with gentleness,
In a new creature, in Your nearness.

Father, may this nation be filled with gentleness,
Men and women, children, in their entirety, no less.
In Your grace, may we be led,
To see You, rejoice before You, in eternal stead.

May we walk with  gentle heart , shun abuse,
In our words and actions, let gentleness appear.
Father, guide us in Your ways,
In gentleness and love, all our days."

# Kamala's Dawn
## A Plea for Divine Obedience

In dawn's quiet, heart tender, Kamala kneels,
Her prayers to render, to God appeals.
"O Father Heavenly, hear our plea,
For self, my children, and our country.

Your commandments all, we acknowledge, sundry,
Striving to follow, with hands steady.
Blessedness from path undefiled, does flow,
Walking in Your law, O Divine Child.

Obedience perfect, not partial, we seek,
Though humble we are, and flesh is weak.
Help us, O Lord of Lords, avoid stain,
On our conscience, or character's main.

To be pure, not spotted, we wish,
In obedience steadfast, sure, like fish.
In all Your commandments divine, we walk,
With hearts wholly Thine, O King of Kings.

Guide us, strengthen us, in this endeavor,
Your doctrine to adorn, failing never.
Grieving not Your Spirit, but bringing joy,
In faith's walk, O Prince of Peace, employ.

May Your grace guide us, as we strive,
In obedience to walk, all our lives.
In Your holy name, O God Almighty,
We end this prayer, with hope brightly. Amen."

# Kamala's Children's
## *Supplication For Journey*

*Dear Heavenly Father, here we stand before You,*
*as children of Kamala,*


In the arena of politics, her true strength does lie,
Tested and challenged, under the nation's watchful eye.
In her journey to win, she may be emotionally scarred,
Yet, with our unwavering support, her resolve is unbarred.


Like states united, not drawn   to discord's call,
Her leadership, too, has a hopeful predawn.
The opposition may hear, may heed the people's plea,
But its fierce nature, it cannot easily decree.


Can opposition be tamed, its ferocity shed?
Yet, between it and her, a line is led.
Distinct in purpose, a line deep and vast,
Separates her from them, ties her to her steadfast past.


Her power of mind, her spirit, are not bound,
Yet in her journey, she is tightly wound.
Amidst the fallen, she finds the will,
To seek wisdom's light, her heart to fulfill.
So here we stand, a humble plea we make,
For divine guidance, for our mother's sake.
Draw her to You, let Your Spirit guide,
In Your holy presence, let her soul confide.


For like the states, she yearns for unity's green,
In Your loving mercy, let her efforts be seen.

And like the opposition, her nature she cannot deny,
Yet for Your grace, oh Lord, she sighs.

In this inability, let Your strength be found,
In her weakness, let Your love resound.
Draw her to You, oh Wisdom, let her be,
In Your holy presence, forever free.
May our supplication find favor in Your sight, oh Lord. Amen.

# Epilogue

This book, "And She Arose as a Mother," is a tribute to the power of motherhood, as exemplified by Kamala Harris and all women. It is not intended to be a political commentary or an endorsement of any particular political ideology. Instead, it explores the universally admired and respected qualities of womanhood and motherhood - love, sacrifice, resilience, and loyalty.

The narrative draws inspiration from the public life and career of Kamala Harris, but it is not a biography. It does not delve into her personal life or pass judgment on her private decisions. Rather, it focuses on her public persona and her role as a mother figure in American politics.

The book also acknowledges the diversity of motherhood. It recognizes that mothers come in many forms - biological mothers, adoptive mothers, foster mothers, and others who step into the role of a mother. Each of these forms of motherhood is celebrated and honored in this book.

The book is designed to motivate and encourage. It honors mothers' resilience and dedication and acknowledges their significant influence in forming our society. It is hoped that readers will find in it a source of inspiration and a beacon of hope.

In writing this book, the intention was not to idealize or idolize Kamala Harris but to highlight the qualities that make her a symbol of motherhood. While this book acknowledges the existence of flaws and shortcomings, it chooses not to concentrate on them. Instead, it highlights the positive attributes that serve to inspire and motivate individuals.

In conclusion, "And She Arose as a Mother" is an ode to mothers everywhere, using the journey of Kamala Harris as a guiding light. It is a testament to the power of motherhood and a tribute to the mothers who shape our world. It is hoped to inspire, uplift, and celebrate mothers in all their diverse forms. It is an apologia for the book, a defense of its purpose and intentions, and a celebration of its subject - the power and beauty of womanhood.

# Acknowledgements

First and foremost, I would like to express my deepest gratitude to Presidential Nominee Kamala Harris, whose life and career have been a source of inspiration for this book. Her dedication to public service, her unwavering commitment to justice, and her embodiment of womanhood have been a guiding light throughout the writing process.

I am also immensely grateful to all the women who have shared their stories and experiences, providing invaluable insights into the diverse forms of womanhood. Their courage, resilience, and strength have been a constant source of inspiration.

I would like to thank my family and friends for their unwavering support and encouragement throughout the writing process. Their belief in the importance of this project has been a driving force behind its completion.

I am grateful to the countless authors, journalists, and scholars whose work has informed and enriched this book. Their rigorous research and insightful analysis have provided a solid foundation for exploring the themes of womanhood and leadership.

I would also like to acknowledge the team of editors, designers, and publishers who have worked tirelessly to bring this book to life. Their expertise and dedication have been instrumental in shaping the final product.

Finally, I would like to express my gratitude to you, the reader, for embarking on this journey with us. Your interest and engagement are the ultimate validation of our efforts. It is my sincere hope that

this book will inspire, uplift, and celebrate women in all their diverse forms.

Thank you for being a part of this journey. Here's to the power and beauty of womanhood!

# About Amma

Amma, an accomplished author with several  books on family, marriage, the Holy Spirit and children, brings forth this book as a powerful reflection on the profound influence of women as mothers of their nation. This book is a heartfelt collection of poems that pay tribute to every woman who aspires to make a positive impact on humanity.

This book is not just about womanhood, but it also highlights the leadership role women play through their maternal influence. It underscores the idea that women, with their nurturing nature and inherent strength, have the potential to shape the future of the next generation.

Amma's dedication extends beyond writing. She is committed to providing inspiration, comfort, advocacy, guidance, wisdom, and spiritual advice to individuals at all stages of life. This commitment aligns with the Christian ethos and the principles of the Paraclete Family.

This book is more than just a collection of poems. It is a valuable resource, a labor of love from Amma. The book serves as a reminder of the power and potential of womanhood. It celebrates the strength,

resilience, and nurturing spirit of women, and their ability to effect change in the world.

It is Amma's hope that this book will resonate with readers, especially women, and inspire them to embrace their unique strengths and make a positive impact in their own lives and the lives of others. Whether you received this book as a gift, borrowed it, or bought it yourself, Amma is delighted that you chose to read it. She values your engagement with her work and welcomes your feedback and criticism, viewing them as opportunities for growth and improvement.

# Email me at

I cordially invite you to share your personal experiences and insights on how the dialogues in "And She Arose" have influenced your life or someone you know. Your feedback is invaluable to me. Please don't hesitate to email Amma at ammagrace98@gmail.com.

I am committed to reminding everyone that they are cherished by God. My mission is to ensure that every person recognizes and feels God's unconditional love for them. I am confident that this understanding will naturally lead me to reciprocate His love.

As our understanding of divine love grows, our faith strengthens, and our commitment to accommodating one another  correctly and loving each other  deepens. All these responsibilities, mutual love, and respect serve as a testament to the world that we are all  indeed part of one Family originating from one race.

I pray for God's grace to guide us so that the very essence of our being is compelled to surrender our  heart to God, fostering godly human relationships, marriages, and parenting. I believe that we can build a world through all our  resources where responsibility, love, unity, and mutual respect are the norm. Thank you for being a part of this journey with me.

# Appendix


Harris, Kamala. (2019). The Truths We Hold: An American Journey. Penguin Press.

CNN. (2018). Judiciary confirmation hearings for Supreme Court nominee Justice Brett Kavanaugh.

ABC News. (2019). Good Morning America interview with Kamala Harris.

Ford, Gerald. (1989). Visit to the Herbert Hoover Presidential Library and Museum.

KAMALA SPEAKS: Sen. Harris Confirms She's Quitting 2020 Race, Vows to 'Help Defeat Donald Trump' - Hannity.com News - Hannity Community. https://community.hannity.com/t/kamala-speaks-sen-harris-confirms-she-s-quitting-2020-race-vows-to-help-defeat-donald-trump/223012

Burt, Richard R. "Strength and Strategy: U.S. Security in the 1990s." The Washington Quarterly, 1988, https://doi.org/10.1080/01636608809477482.

Visit the Herbert Hoover Presidential Library and Museum | National Archives. https://www.archives.gov/presidential-libraries/visit/hoover.html